With a unique combination of pastoral wisdom, clear practical advice and personal reflection, the contagious passion of *Compelled by Joy* will refuel and equip you to spread the good news with delight. Michael has set down in words the wisdom of a lifetime laid down for the Lord: a beautiful gift to us who are striving to tread the same narrow path.
Lydia Allister, RZIM Europe Associate

A sparkling book – a gem and a treasure – just like the author! Written by one of the most remarkable evangelists God has given to the global church in these past fifty years, it is full of wit, wisdom and experience. No reader could fail to be touched by the profound enthusiasm and love for the gospel, as well as for the Christ of the gospel, exhibited in the writings of Michael Green. Be prepared to be enthused, encouraged and energized as you read this book.
Lindsay Brown, Evangelist-at-Large, IFES; International Director, Lausanne Movement for World Evangelization

A thoroughly stimulating book on the Christian faith which combines the freshness of a seeker after truth with the penetration of a scholar, which he undoubtedly is! It did my heart good to read it.
Lord George Carey, 103rd Archbishop of Canterbury, 1991–2002

Michael Green is one of the most effective evangelists the UK has produced and is also a fine theologian, pastor and apologist. He manages to blend all these skills together in this gem of a book. These life-lessons and reflections will motivate and equip you (as they have me) to live and speak for Jesus with renewed urgency, effectiveness and joy.
Richard Cunningham, Director UCCF: The Christian Unions

Michael Green has been a model, motivator and mentor to me for three decades. *Compelled by Joy* is full of inspirational insights and a wealth of wisdom distilled over many years.
Canon J. John, author and evangelist

Michael Green is an international treasure. Every page in *Compelled by Joy* is passionate, provocative and prophetic – just like the author! Michael shares wisdom he has gained over a lifetime as one of the most effective evangelists in the world today. This isn't a book only for evangelists – but for anyone who has ever struggled with knowing how to talk about sin or how to share the gospel in a fresh yet faithful way. *Compelled by Joy* is a wake-up call to the church passionately to communicate God's glorious gospel to a world in desperate need of Good News.
Rebecca Manley Pippert, author of Out of the Salt Shaker *and* Hope Has Its Reasons

Conviction, joy and courage are words that I associate with Michael Green. He has lived a joy-filled life centred on making Jesus Christ known, and it is a privilege to commend this book as a must-read for anyone wanting to win others for Christ.
Amy Orr-Ewing, UK Director of RZIM Europe

Compelled by Joy lives up to its title. It is a joy to read. Passionate, informed, authentic, biblical, inspiring and practical. The veteran evangelist Michael Green draws on his long experience, but shows his cutting edge is as sharp as ever. It will restore any flagging confidence in the gospel and reinvigorate zeal for evangelism. I will buy this book to give to many of my friends to spur them on in their task of making Jesus known.
Derek Tidball, formerly Principal of London School of Theology, and currently Visiting Scholar at Spurgeon's College, London

Sunil & Sally

Compelled by Joy

A lifelong passion for evangelism

Michael Green

Michael Green

Compelled by Joy

Joy

A lifelong passion for evangelism

ivp

INTER-VARSITY PRESS
Norton Street, Nottingham NG7 3HR, England
Email: ivp@ivpbooks.com
Website: www.ivpbooks.com

First published 2011

British Library Cataloguing in Publication Data
A catalogue record for this book is available from the British Library.

ISBN: 978–1–84474–542–5

Set in Adobe Garamond 12/15pt
Typeset in Great Britain by CRB Associates, Potterhanworth, Lincolnshire
Printed and bound in Great Britain by Ashford Colour Press Ltd, Gosport,
Hampshire

*Inter-Varsity Press publishes Christian books that are true to the Bible and that
communicate the gospel, develop discipleship and strengthen the church for its mission
in the world.*

*Inter-Varsity Press is closely linked with the Universities and Colleges Christian
Fellowship, a student movement connecting Christian Unions in universities and
colleges throughout Great Britain, and a member movement of the International
Fellowship of Evangelical Students. Website: www.uccf.org.uk*

For my friends
Carrie Boren, Arkan Zaki, Sandy McEachern,
Kristopher Bate, and Mary Jane Axelson,
graduates of the Oxford Centre for Christian Apologetics
and their generation of evangelists

CONTENTS

Chapter 1

THE TREASURE AND THE PASSION

This morning I read these words from the Bible:

His word is in my heart like a fire,
  a fire shut up in my bones.
I am weary of holding it in;
  indeed, I cannot.
(Jeremiah 20:9)

And I knew then what I must do. I had been approached by the publishers to write a book on 'reflections of a lifelong evangelist', and I had been wondering whether or not to do it. I would hesitate no longer.

As by definition this is to be a personal book, recording my own reflections on the subject of evangelism, perhaps I should begin by saying that I am not altogether happy with the name 'evangelist'. It is at once too misleading and too restrictive. Misleading because the word can mean so many things to

different people. A fanatic with a one-track mind. A shallow,
narrow-minded enthusiast, quite possibly on the make. A person
obsessed with the Bible, a book written at least two millennia
ago. An illiberal bore, out to change other people's opinions.
An obscurantist with outdated views on absolute truth. And no
doubt you can add to those impressions. They make it abundantly clear that there is no one single received understanding
of what is meant by an evangelist. It is a misleading word.

The term is restrictive too. It does not tell you who I
am: a husband, father, grandfather and sports enthusiast.
I am both an academic and a pastor, both driven and lazy,
both humble and proud, both sociable and reclusive. I am a
mixture. We all are. But at the core of that confused muddle
which is myself, there is a passion burning. It has been
burning away since my late teens, sometimes brightly,
sometimes smouldering dully. It is simply this: I have found
treasure – by no skill of my own – and I want to share it as
widely as I can.

The imagery is not mine. I found it in a short parable of
Jesus Christ. He tells of a farm labourer, ploughing away in
his field, no doubt bored and with little expectancy. Perhaps
he was thinking of his lunch. He might even have been thinking
ahead to some sort of a crop months later. And then suddenly
his ploughshare strikes an obstacle. He bends down to see what
it is. It turns out to be a casket, containing buried treasure.
Imagine his delight as he holds up the pearls and rubies to the
sunlight, and as he savours the heavy gold coins in his hands.
He has found treasure, and he is willing to sell everything he
has in order to become the owner of that field – and of that
treasure (Matthew 13:44–45).

Jesus matched this arresting story with a companion piece that was at once very similar and very different. It told of a pearl fancier who travelled in search of the very best pearls in the world. And one day he came across a pearl which eclipsed every other one he had ever seen. He quite simply had to acquire that pearl. So he sold everything to get it.

Both stories tell of an amazing discovery. Both tell of the lengths individuals were prepared to go to in order to gain the treasure and the pearl. But whereas one was searching for it diligently, the other came across it by accident. It is not hard to see that Jesus Christ is the treasure in both short stories. He is that pearl of great price. He is so attractive that it is worth dropping every goal in order to get in touch with him. And whereas some people have been searching for that fulfilment all their lives, others come across it by accident.

I was in the latter category. I was a happy teenager, content with my home, my academic success, my sporting prowess and my friendships. And I stumbled across the greatest friendship of all: that with Jesus Christ. He is the treasure that I have come to value above all else. I was not an emotional cripple looking for a crutch. I was not a romantic looking for a cause. I was not at the bottom of the pile hoping for a leg-up. I was not looking for anything in particular in fact. But I found treasure. That treasure has utterly transformed my life, my goals, my lifestyle. And that is the source of my passion, to share the treasure with others.

Before anyone dismisses this as religious nonsense, let me emphasize that religion is not the treasure. Religion has been responsible for many of the ills of humankind, as atheists are not slow to point out. Nor is churchgoing the treasure.

Churchgoing can be deadly boring, as I found out for myself over a period of a good few years. Ceremonies are not the treasure. I was baptized as an infant and confirmed as a teenager, but that made no difference to my lifestyle. It was certainly not treasure. Neither was ethical behaviour. That was frankly boring as well. Who likes the goody-goody?

None of these things was the treasure. *Jesus was.*

Let me tell you how I discovered him, or rather how he laid hold of me. I was a teenager at Clifton College in Bristol, and was invited by a friend to a surreptitious meeting in the school cricket pavilion one Sunday afternoon. There I found some forty boys, listening attentively to the Professor of Surgery at Bristol University, who also I discovered edited the *British Medical Journal.* He was talking about Jesus Christ. And to my astonishment he spoke with quiet conviction that Jesus was alive, and that it was possible to know him! This was revolutionary to me. I knew a fair amount about Jesus. He had been the background warmth to my growing up. I had read the Gospels, and had even won a prize on them. But nobody had ever told me that Jesus was still alive, and could make a real difference to our lives. Yet here was this highly intelligent scientist, who not only believed it and lived in the light of it, but thought it sufficiently important to give up his valuable time on a Sunday afternoon to instruct a bunch of schoolboys on it!

This set me thinking. If this professor and the group of boys into which I had unwittingly tumbled were correct, then they had made the most important discovery of all time. If they were wrong, then I need not trouble myself further with Christianity. It would prove to be merely a matter of following the ideals and teaching of a revered but dead teacher, and that should not make any serious impact on my life.

I resolved to find out whether or not they were right. So I set out to do two things. I would regularly attend the meeting of these Jesus enthusiasts and see what I made of the teaching. And I would watch their way of life with some care, to see if their profession of faith made any difference. The question of whether Jesus was really risen and relevant was the most important issue one could consider. It was quite literally the key to the meaning of existence. I was determined not to be taken for a ride. I needed to examine it carefully for myself.

So I watched the members of this meeting over the course of the next nine months or so. I was impressed by the way they conducted themselves. I was equally impressed by the teaching given at these meetings: so clear, so biblical, so sensible and accessible. It was worlds away from the content of school chapel which, in those far-off days, we were obliged to attend daily. I could no longer resist the claim that Jesus was alive. From an investigator I had over those months turned into a seeker. I was now convinced that this stuff was true. I realized that it was all to do with Jesus. But to me he was still the stained-glass-window Jesus, the Stranger of Galilee encased in dusty books of the New Testament. And I was fed up with religion. I was hungry for reality.

So one Sunday I went up to Richard Gorrie, the mature senior boy who led the meeting. He was only nineteen, but had a wisdom beyond his years. I asked him a dumb question. He saw through me, and I think he must have recognized that I was ready to embark on the adventure of faith. We went to

the upstairs storey in that cricket pavilion, and he led me
to Christ. I found treasure!

I cannot recall all the details of that Sunday afternoon. But
the main outlines are burnt into my memory. As we sat together
on a bench, I can see in my mind's eye the cricket bats and pads,
the spikes in the boots and the divots of dried turf on the heavily
scored floor. I remember him gently pointing out to me how I
had offended God by my way of life. I could not argue. He had,
only the term before, been obliged as head boy to give me a
richly deserved punishment for illegal entry into his house at
the school. I knew my life was a mess. I could not keep my
language clean for more than a sentence or two. I was violent
with other people. My friends and I made gunpowder to explode
in inappropriate places, and burnt down huts in order to obtain
the necessary carbon. Yes, I knew I could not look a holy God
in the face. I did not need to have that truth rubbed in.

But then Richard showed me something that I had never
seen before. He showed me that Jesus Christ had done all that
was necessary to bring me back to God. On the cross he had
taken responsibility for all the dark side of my life. I already
believed in a vague way that Christ had died for the sins of the
world. After all, it came across in almost every service I
attended. But it had never meant anything much to me. That
afternoon I saw that he had died for me personally, bearing
responsibility for all my failures and deliberate wrong actions.
It was the evil in me, and in others, that had held him on that
cruel cross. He had gone there willingly, out of his great love.

I recall that Richard gave me a graphic illustration of the
difference Calvary had made. He used the prophecy of Isaiah
53, and illustrated the phrase 'We all, like sheep, have gone

astray' by placing a black object between his left hand and the light. That represented the responsibility for my misdeeds resting on me, cutting me off from the light and the warmth of God's holy love. 'Each of us has turned to his own way,' the verse continued. I could not quarrel with that. I knew it was true. 'And the LORD has laid on him the iniquity of us all,' continued my friend, transferring the dark load to his other hand, which stood for Christ dying on the cross. Of course, this released the left hand, which represented me. No longer did there need to be a 'cloud of unknowing' to separate me from God. In that ancient prophecy, pointing so clearly to the cross, I saw for the first time in my life that Christ had carried away my burden of evil; he had taken personal responsibility for all my offences. The whole revolting lot was poured on his sinless head, and he accepted it voluntarily so that I could go free.

I am not ashamed to admit that such sacrificial love broke me down. I thought I was tough. But I wept.

And that was not all. My second shock that afternoon was occasioned by Richard's gentle question: whether or not I believed that Jesus Christ had risen from the grave. That was the question, of course, which had started my search. By now I was satisfied that it was true, and told Richard as much. He then faced me with a crunch question: 'Very well, if so, what are you going to do about him?' I began dimly to see that I was faced by a massive choice. Either I could walk away from the one who had loved me and given himself for me, or I could yield my whole life, my future, to this risen Christ. There was no middle way. I was on the horns of a dilemma. I had to choose.

That led to my third discovery that memorable afternoon.
I must have told him that I had no idea how to respond to the
magnitude of what God in Christ had done for me. So he took
me to a verse in the Bible which has led millions to a personal
faith. It was Revelation 3:20, where the risen and ascended
Christ says these wonderful words to a lukewarm church,
lukewarm because they had kept him excluded from their
church and their personal lives. 'Here I am! I stand at the door
and knock. If anyone hears my voice and opens the door, I
will come in and eat with him, and he with me.'

Though there was much that I did not understand, the heart
of the matter was now clear enough. The Jesus who had dealt
with the barrier that seemed to make God so far away, the Jesus
who had smashed the power of the Last Enemy by the great
victory of Easter Day – this Jesus, the Son of the living God,
was alive and could be met personally. He was willing to enter
my life by means of his Holy Spirit. Of course, Christ himself
had returned to heaven at the ascension, but I do not recall
that this posed any problem to me. He was apparently willing,
indeed enthusiastic, to place his unseen Spirit in my life, and
start living in me. So it would no longer be just me, but myself
and the Spirit of Christ. What an exciting, if daunting,
prospect! It was undreamed-of generosity for God to act like
that. However, it would be very demanding. It would call for
the clearing up of the mess in my life. I could not achieve this
by myself. I had tried, repeatedly, but in vain. I hoped that
Christ might be able to do it, but I realized that I had to be
willing for a revolution to start within me. My sins were
comfortable. Like ivy on a tree, they had been intertwined
with my life for many years. It would be hard to break free of

them. And it would mean that Jesus, not I, was henceforth to be the one who would call the shots in my life, my behaviour, my ambitions, my relationships. Was I prepared for such a costly takeover? What is more, I knew I would not be able to keep quiet about this overwhelming discovery. I would have to be willing to 'let my light shine', as the Gospels put it, and once I knew a bit more, I would need to be Christ's vocal ambassador as well.

How much I understood of all this that Sunday afternoon I do not know. But I know I counted the cost of discipleship as best I could.

Richard helped me to see what needed to be done by showing me a postcard of Holman Hunt's famous painting, *The Light of the World*. It had been inspired by Revelation 3:20, and shows Christ clad in dazzling white, and with a blood-red cloak, standing outside the door of a dark and desolate cottage. In his hand he holds a lantern – is he not the Light of the World? Clearly he is looking for access, and then the light will illuminate all the house and shine out of the windows. But equally clearly he will not enter until he is invited. The door is choked by ivy: it has never been opened. Yet patiently Christ stands knocking, with the nail marks in his hand. He is waiting to be invited in. He is offering to come in and stay for ever. The imagery was lucid and compelling.

That afternoon I gladly and deliberately accepted Christ's offer. I did so with gratitude (yes, with tears as well: tears from a tough male in mid-teens, tears that hit the dust on the floor and bounced). I blurted out my response to him in prayer, and I am grateful that I was encouraged to begin my active discipleship with an audible prayer. Many church people spend fifty years and more in church, and yet seem unable to pray out loud. It has no particular merit, of course, apart from concentrating your thoughts and enabling others to share in your petitions. But that in itself is not unimportant.

Before we left that cricket pavilion, my friend gave me some immediate aftercare. He told me how to meet the initial doubts that would inevitably come. To begin with, I would have no experience to depend on, but I had the promise of Christ who could not break his word. If he said, 'I will come in', and I had asked him, then he *had* come in. I could rely on his promise. That was a great help to me in the early days of discipleship. It is, after all, one of the basic aspects of faith: believing the promises of God and resting my weight on them.

Richard then tried to introduce me to a rudimentary devotional life. He suggested that for this I should forthwith get up at 7.10 am when the first rising bell rang in the school house I belonged to. There was a second bell at 7.25, and all boys had to be on parade for 'call-over' at 7.30 (on pain of caning for three absences!). Those of us with some bravado made a point of not stirring before the second bell went. Indeed, I never used even to hear the first bell. When I told Richard this, he was somewhat nonplussed, but responded very wisely, 'Ask the Lord to wake you up at the first bell, and then get up and spend a bit of time with your Bible and in prayer before the day gets underway.' I was prepared to give it a try. And to my amazement, I found that I did wake up – and get up – the next morning at 7.10, and continued to do so every morning for the rest of my time at the school. Those fifteen minutes or so before call-over, in the privacy of a loo, proved invaluable for getting me into the habit of devotional

Bible reading and prayer. I remember I started reading Romans. I had never been able to make head or tail of the Epistles before my conversion, but now they began to resonate with my new life in Christ.

Before I left that afternoon, Richard encouraged me to start informal prayer: to talk to the Lord as I went along the road back to my house. I did not need to shut my eyes or kneel down. I had encountered the Friend 'who sticks closer than a brother' (Proverbs 18:24), and it would become the most natural thing in the world to speak to him, and listen to him, at any time and on any topic. In this way, I began to learn how to remain close to Christ and to live my life with growing awareness of his companionship.

There were two particular ways in which Richard Gorrie was of further help to me. In the first place, he invited me to a Christian house party for boys in the holidays. I saw that this would be a way to develop my Christian life, and enthusiastically agreed to go. That house party became an important part of my adolescent and young adult life. I learnt a relevant and attractive pattern of Christian discipleship among boys of my own age, specifically related to life in a boarding school. And when in due course I became an undergraduate and began to help in the leadership of this house party, I found I was given marvellous training. Indeed, in three areas I have never met anything superior: how to give an attractive talk, how to lead an inductive Bible study, and how to engage in basic pastoral work. All this lay in the future, but I know that the friendships, worship, fun and teaching of this holiday house party and term-time school meeting were an enormous help to me in the formative period of my Christian life.

The other help Richard afforded me was this: he made himself available about once a fortnight to answer any questions and objections I had about the Christian life. I used to make a note of some of them as they cropped up, and would save them to talk over with him. He would then answer them to my satisfaction, and choose a short passage of the New Testament to read with me, and show me how to draw out thoughts from Scripture for my own life. This personal mentoring is sadly missing in many parts of the Christian world today, and it is immensely valuable. I might well have foundered without it.

No profession of Christian faith has validity unless it produces a change of life. You may wonder what differences, if any, began to emerge in me. In fact they were fairly visible, because, as I've said before, I had been quite a high-profile troublemaker. One difference was my language. I found that the habits of swearing and obscenity, which had held me in such a tight grip, disappeared almost overnight. I remember praying with the psalmist, 'Set a guard over my mouth, O LORD; keep watch over the door of my lips' (Psalm 141:3). To my amazement, within a few weeks every trace of swearing and obscenity was gone, and they have never returned since. The other thing was my violent temper. I was a passable boxer, and I used violence on people outside the ring as well as in it, when my Welsh temper would flare up. But once I had entrusted my life to Christ and asked him to work on this problem, I found that I did not even want to hit people. That change too has remained.

I do not mention these two failings because I think they are particularly important, but because they mattered to me, and I had found myself quite unable to get rid of them before. Yet the power of Christ made short work of both. This was an enormous encouragement to me. I think that God often gives graphic and immediate answers to prayer in the early days of our Christian lives to help us get started in trusting him. Later on, answers seem to be much slower and more gradual. Progress in Christlikeness is a tortuous business because of the battle between the old life and the new. But despite the ups and downs, we can expect to experience gradual progress, though in this life there will always be a long way to go. It is only when we see him as he is that we shall be made like him, so St John assures us (1 John 3:2), and that will not be until eternity.

During the remaining years at school, my Christian life saw solid growth. I began to try to please Christ in every aspect of my life, probably becoming for a while unnecessarily narrow in what I allowed myself, but maybe that was a good failing. I found I was becoming very keen to share the joy of this treasure I had discovered with others who seemed every bit as blind to it as I had been. Naturally I was not competent to help them to faith myself yet, and in any case that would have been politically unacceptable within the closely bound network of an English public school. But I was able to invite them to the same house party which had been such a help to me, and I had the joy of seeing a number of them becoming firmly committed Christians as a result. I guess that is where the seeds of evangelism were sown in my heart. They have persisted, and indeed grown, ever since.

I have explained at some length how the passion for evangelism arose in my own life. It started at the cross, when I came face to face with Jesus Christ, saw what he had done for me and what he offered me, and entrusted my life to him.

Soon the Jesus whose Spirit had entered my life began to induce in me some frail reflection of the concern for others which had marked his own ministry, and had driven him out like a shepherd to rescue lost sheep. He said that he had come to seek and to save the lost, and his ministry showed it at every turn. I began to share in that passion.

I recall one Bible passage that a number of us were looking at, which made an indelible impression on me. It was 2 Corinthians 4:1ff., where the apostle Paul speaks of his own passion for evangelism, and mentions one of the powerful motives that lay behind it. 'If our gospel is veiled,' he writes, 'it is veiled to those who are perishing. The god of this age has blinded the minds of unbelievers, so that they cannot see the light of the gospel of the glory of Christ, who is the image of God' (4:3–4). It struck me very forcibly. I realized that I had been blinded: I had been quite unable to see the attractiveness of the gospel of Christ. I began to recognize that there was an anti-God force choreographing that blindness, while God was longing to remove it. I saw that my friends, my intelligent, delightful, sporting friends were just as blind as I had been, and were in danger of perishing for lack of the good news that had come my way. And the passion mastered me. Paul exclaimed, 'God, who said, "Let light shine out of darkness," made his light shine in our hearts to give us the light of the knowledge of the glory of God in the face of Christ' (2 Corinthians 4:6). Yes, the face of Jesus Christ had indeed shone his light into my heart.

Although, as the apostle continues, 'we have this treasure in jars of clay' (4:7), frail human beings that we are, I could not help myself saying an enthusiastic 'Yes' to his conclusion:

'Therefore we do not lose heart' (4:16). He uses that phrase twice in the chapter, reminding his readers of God's mercy to them, and the great privilege that he has entrusted this ministry of evangelism to them: so 'we do not lose heart.' The word means 'to back off', 'to play the coward'. Paul had every reason to lose heart, in the face of all the hardships that faced him throughout his tempestuous career. Yet he did not lose heart. My resolve was that I would not lose heart either. All those years ago, I wanted to be involved in passing on the treasure of Jesus Christ as long as I live. That is still my desire.

Chapter 2

GOD IS NOT MONOLITHIC

Because these are my own reflections about evangelism, I have inevitably spent some time explaining how I came to the living faith which I am passionate about passing on. But it would be a great mistake to suppose that everybody comes to Christ in a similar way. This is obviously not the case. Nor would it be appropriate for the God who is so varied in his self-revelation in the natural world to be boringly monolithic in the spiritual world. God is sovereign, and he has countless different ways of drawing human beings into relationship with himself – though, as we shall see, there are always some constants. In this chapter we will explore both.

The variety of God's approach and call

Preaching
Some people come to Christ through direct preaching. For many years I was rector of St Aldate's, a large church in Oxford,

where we saw scores of students every year entering into a committed Christian faith as a result of the evangelistic preaching which was a feature of the church. It helped, of course, that the vast majority of the 800 or more who crowded in to the church on Sunday mornings were themselves students in their twenties. To see fellow students piling into church aroused the curiosity of new students, whose previous impression had been that Christianity was only suitable for the very old or the very stupid. It helped too to have dynamic worship, testimony to the difference Christ makes (offered from time to time by members of the congregation) and the judicious use of drama and dance. This was not the old traditional service that they had long ago deserted, if they had ever encountered it at all. Its format was relevant and up to date, but at its heart lay preaching, and it was not at all unusual for twenty or more individuals to come forward at the end of an evangelistic service, profoundly touched by what they had heard, and resolved to give their lives to Christ. If the preaching was scriptural and relevant to the situation of the hearers, there was almost always a decisive response. Sometimes people would come in halfway through the service, having had no intention of being there – they were passing by and just felt constrained to enter. Many times I have seen such people, who an hour or two earlier had no thought of God in their minds, surrender to Christ after an encounter with him in the sermon.

Only today I have been spending time with a man who was a convinced atheist until the age of forty, had never entered a church in his life, and then did so on one occasion, heard the gospel, walked out of the church a different man, and is now about to be ordained in the Church of England following training! There is a strange power in Scripture. 'The word of God is living and active, sharper than any double-edged sword . . . ', according to the letter to the Hebrews (4:12), and we certainly found it to be so.

Preaching is such a mystery. As I have stood time and again in the pulpit at St Aldate's Church, I have seen one person in tears of repentance under the impact of the preached word, sitting next to another who is quite untouched, and is simply looking at his watch. It certainly is not merely human eloquence. God seems to have imparted a power to biblical preaching, which goes straight to the heart of some, though not all.

Sacraments

Some people come into active Christian faith through the sacraments which Jesus left us, primarily baptism and Holy Communion. This should occasion no surprise, since Jesus himself ordained these sacraments to be the powerful signs and symbols of the new life: baptism pointing to its inauguration, and Communion to its continuance. Consequently, throughout Christian history, although baptism has seemed an apparently meaningless ceremony for many, millions of people would attribute the start of their Christian lives to their baptism. I guess this should be the normal thing, particularly if we are talking about believers' baptism. What could be more powerful than an immersion in the name of the Triune God? You die to the old life as you go beneath the waters, and you rise to new life in Christ as you emerge. The ancient church designed baptistries to make this plain, with steps cut in the

stonework for you to descend into the water on one side of
the baptistry and stairs to ascend on the other. They gave the
new believer milk and honey as a mark of entering the land of
promise, and they clothed him or her with a white garment
to denote their status as fully accepted before God.

I recall a mission in London which included an evangelistic
address by myself in a strongly Anglo-Catholic church. The
powers that be were planning to have 'asperges' in the service,
a sprinkling of the congregation with water in memory of their
baptism, and to awaken them afresh to its significance and
claim on their lives. Talking over with the rector beforehand
how we could combine this with an evangelistic talk, we agreed
that I would conclude my challenge with an invitation to any
who had not been baptized, but wanted to entrust their lives
to Christ in the light of what they had heard, to come forward
and be baptized then and there. Five did so, and there was
great rejoicing as we turned to sprinkle the rest of the congregation with baptismal water! But this instant baptism was so
shocking to some of the clerics gathered there, that they sternly
rebuked the incumbent and reported me to the bishop, who
fortunately had the good sense to take no action. I was merely
doing what the first preachers of the gospel did, baptize
immediately on profession of faith. I gather that each of those
five went on in the Christian life, despite what many churchmen
would see as their irregular initiation!

Not only baptism but the Eucharist or Lord's Supper, the
great Christian thanksgiving meal for the death of the Lord
Jesus, can be the start of active Christian commitment. I recall
a bizarre occasion once when I was rector of St Aldate's. There
was such a crush of people attending that we used to pass the

bread and wine down the rows so that people could administer them to one another. On this occasion, I saw an undergraduate shaking his head and passing the bread and cup on to his neighbour. I pushed my way into the row and asked him, 'Have you entrusted your life to Christ yet?' He replied, 'Not yet, but I am thinking about it.' 'Well, now is the best of all times to do so,' I replied. 'See, here are the most powerful symbols of Christ's death on the cross for you personally. He shed his precious blood for you. Come to him right now!' And the man then and there cried out to the Lord for mercy. At once I said to people further down the row, 'Pass the bread and wine back for our friend to partake', and partake he did joyfully and became a thoroughly wholehearted Christian.

An equally bizarre example of the power of Christ encountering people through the Eucharist comes from a dynamic clergyman I met a few years ago. He had been a thoroughgoing atheist, though well enough disposed to the local vicar to do occasional repair jobs on the external structure of the church building. However, he never went in. But one evening he decided that he would. It was an entirely silent High Church service of Benediction, in which the sacramental bread and wine are exposed to view so that the congregation can, through them, worship Christ. Without a word being spoken, his life was turned around, and he became not only a keen Christian, but a most effective clergyman! To be sure, God is not monolithic. He has many different ways of drawing people to his Son.

Healing and deliverance

There are times when God spectacularly intervenes in the regular course of events to heal people. Of course, the normal way in which this happens is through medicine, but God sometimes shortcuts the process.

I remember encountering this for the first time when I was a newly ordained minister. In our youth group there was a young man with his leg in callipers. He could not walk properly, and he could not read either, for that matter. Well, he went away to a Pentecostal weekend where his leg was fully restored, and his callipers were no longer needed. Not surprisingly, he came to faith and began to learn to read because he so much wanted to read the Bible. That taught me something I had not learned in theological college! But since then I have seen such things happen again and again. God does sometimes break through to heal, and people do sometimes come to explicit Christian faith through a healing. One of my current students from a Middle East country left Islam to become a Christian when his mother was completely healed from cancer in answer to prayer.

It is much the same with the ministry of deliverance. Slow though we are in the West to recognize it, there are dark spiritual forces which infest people's lives, and when those dark forces are expelled by the power of Christ, almost always the grateful recipient becomes a committed Christian. I discovered this first when I was doing some evangelistic meetings in Ghana, early in my life as a minister. I was sitting on a truckle bed next to a strong young Ghanaian woman who had reached the point of decision and had asked Christ to come and save her. Immediately she fell right across me (to my embarrassment!), completely unconscious. I did not know what to do, so I just prayed the name of Jesus repeatedly, and soon she came round, sat up and confessed Jesus Christ with joy. Christ had set her free from whatever spiritual force was battling against her conversion. Many years later I met her in the USA. She was working for the United Nations, I seem to remember, and she was a radiant Christian.

These things happen in Britain too, though less frequently, in my experience. I think that is because, in our secularized culture, Satan works in a more sophisticated way. Why resort to demonic invasion when you can blind people's eyes with materialism and sex? I recall one remarkable situation in a town-wide mission in the north of England. A couple, obviously disturbed, came up to the Communion rail for ministry after the service. As I prayed for the man, he became violent and obscene. He was clearly under some dark influence, so I rebuked the evil spirit, and he immediately became silent, while his partner broke out with the same violence and obscenities. The spirit had moved from one to the other! In the name of Christ I bound this spirit and sent it away to the place of God's direction. Both partners became believers.

I think of another occasion on a mission when, as people gradually moved out after the evening service, a group of our team gathered around a woman who looked distraught and was making a lot of fuss. I was busy with somebody else, thankful that this particular woman had not come my way. But in due course the team members called me over. I sensed after a while that the problem might well lie in a necklace that she had worn day and night for many years. It had been offered for blessing to a heathen deity. Clearly it was going to be a big battle to break this necklace off, but eventually we did so, and with great joy the woman was released to entrust her life to Christ. We all went out and threw the necklace into the river.

Early next morning I was summoned to her home. Her parents wanted to know how this remarkable restoration of their forty-year-old daughter had happened. I told them, pointing them to the Christ who had made such a graphic difference to their daughter, and both of them fell to their knees in their own sitting room and gave themselves to Christ. I can never forget it. This sort of thing seems so strange to us, but when people have been in bondage to a spiritual force of evil for many years, it is hardly surprising that they turn with great joy to the Christ who sets them free.

Visions and other surprises

It is not universally known in the West, but worldwide many thousands of Muslims come to Christian faith every year. Often they live in countries where Christianity is forbidden. God seems to get through to them by means of visions. This is extremely common in countries such as Pakistan, and the fascinating thing is that people always seem to recognize the person who appears to them in the vision. I recall meeting several Christian leaders in Malaysia who had been brought to Christ by a compelling vision. Visions, healing, testimony and Scripture seem to be the main four ways by which people in countries that have not been exposed to the gospel come to faith.

Sometimes God uses very unusual means to draw people to himself. I think of Professor C. E. M. Joad, from London University, who used to figure prominently in years gone by on the BBC *Brains Trust* programmes. He was an atheist, and made no bones about it. But later in his life he became a committed Christian, and even wrote a book called *Recovery of Belief*, repudiating his previous tenaciously held opinions. What was the reason for this change? He had, in one of his books, used an illustration. How would it be if he travelled on the train without buying a ticket? Well, he was discovered doing that very thing. It caused an outcry at the time, and he was banned from broadcasting. But it was the sheer fact of evil, evil in his own personality, that caused him to reject the liberal humanism in which he had been reared. He threw in his lot with the Jesus who came to break such bondage.

A man even more famous than Professor Joad was W. H. Auden. In 1939 he emigrated to the USA, and shortly after the start of the war he saw a film of Nazi atrocities following their capture of Poland. When Poles appeared on the screen, he was startled to hear people in the cinema shouting, 'Kill them, kill them!' Auden was stunned. He had believed in the essential goodness of humanity. Now in a flash he saw how misguided such a belief was. He realized that, as he put it, 'human nature was not and never could be good'. But if he was to say this, he had to have a standard by which to make such judgments. He left the cinema committed to a search that in due course led him to Christ.

The constant elements in conversion

So our God is not single track in the ways he approaches the diversity of human temperaments. Nevertheless, there are some constants in the launch of Christian discipleship across the spectrum of human personality, and we are given an illuminating example in the New Testament itself.

It would be true to say that, among some modern evangelists at least, the conversion of Saul of Tarsus provides the model of what we should be aiming for. The account of his conversion in Acts 9, and the two personal accounts he gives of it in Acts 22 and 26, reveal four rather clear elements in the change that came to this remarkable man.

One element was that he recognized his need. He was deeply prejudiced against Christians, for reasons which doubtless seemed good to him, and which led to his being a driven man, driven by hatred and the determination to root out this heretical movement, at the cost of prison and death for its adherents. The first hint we are given of his attitude is when we are told that he looked after the clothes of those who stripped off to stone Stephen, the first Christian martyr, to death. Maybe his conscience first began to accuse him when he saw the glory on Stephen's face as he died with a prayer for God's forgiveness for his murderers. At all events, by the time he had that astonishing encounter with Christ on the road to Damascus, we read the divine voice accurately depicting his state: 'It is hard for you to kick against the goads' (Acts 26:14). This was an allusion to ploughing: the farmer used to prick the side of an ox in order to correct the direction it was taking. God was doing the same with Saul of Tarsus.

The second element in his conversion was a measure of understanding. 'Who are you, Lord?' he burst out (26:15), as he had that vision of the ascended Christ. He knew then that Jesus was Lord. That word had a variety of meanings, from 'sir' to 'God'. However he understood it, Paul must have realized that the one he had despised as a failed messianic pretender who perished under the curse of God, crucifixion, was exalted to the highest place in the universe. And 'Lord' became one of his most favoured adjuncts to the name Jesus. It cannot be denied that on the Damascus road Saul had a revolution in his understanding of Jesus. So Jesus was risen from the dead! So he was no failed heretic, but God's special agent of redemption!

The third element in Saul's conversion was an act of surrender. He allowed himself to obey the divine voice. He would get up from the ground to which he had fallen in awe, and enter the city, where it would be made plain to him what he was to do. And so this blazing firebrand for Jewish orthodoxy, now humbled, blinded and disoriented, allowed himself to go and stay in Damascus. We are told that he spent three days, still blinded, in prayer and fasting. Then Ananias, one of the Christians whom he had come to destroy, was guided by God to go and greet Saul now as a Christian brother, and pray for the restoration of his sight and his filling with the Holy Spirit. So this third element in the man's conversion was complex. It involved humbling, obedience to God's voice, prayer, fasting, and waiting for a short period before the restoration of his vision and his filling with the Holy Spirit, together with the glimmering of an understanding of the cost of discipleship and the plan God had for his life. In a word, it meant surrender.

Change, the fourth element in Saul's conversion, began to manifest itself very speedily. That ninth chapter of Acts shows many signs of the new life that was coursing through his being. First, we are told of his close fellowship with the Christian disciples, the very people he had been planning to drag off in chains to the high priest. Then we find him making his first forays into preaching Jesus as the Son of God in the hardest of all places, the Jewish synagogues. We find him growing in confidence and understanding, showing convincing proof that

Jesus was the long-awaited Messiah. Then we find another mark of the new life: opposition. The Jews tried to kill him, but Saul escaped over the city wall, lowered in a basket. Those were some of the immediate marks of the reality of change in the life of Saul.

Four elements in conversion: recognition of need, understanding something about the work of Christ, revolutionary commitment to him, and the proof of it in a transformed life. Is that the way it should happen to everyone, complete with visions, blindness and emotional falling to the ground?

Not so. Nor does Scripture present Saul as the unique model of conversion. Contrast him with the man who dominates the first half of the book of Acts, Simon Peter. When was Simon converted? It is very difficult to answer that question. Was it when Andrew introduced him to Jesus, and he first fell under the spell of this rabbi who saw into his very soul, saying, 'You are Simon, but you will be Peter' (i.e. a man of rock)? Was it when he was the first of the little band of followers of Jesus to confess him as the Son of the living God, at Caesarea Philippi? Was it when he went out and wept bitterly after denying Jesus at his trial? Was it at that personal interview after the resurrection which we find alluded to in Scripture, but never described?

The answer is that we do not know. There was no one sudden moment of illumination from which all else sprang. This should remind us that whereas some come to Christ by an apparently sudden route like Saul of Tarsus, others come by a much more winding and tortuous road. Nevertheless, it is not difficult to discern the very same elements in Peter's conversion, long drawn-out though it may have been, as in that of Saul of Tarsus. Like Saul, Peter came to see the mess of his own life. When he experienced a miraculous catch of fish, as Luke 5 recounts, he fell at Jesus' feet and recognized his sinfulness. It was the same when he went out and wept bitterly after three times denying his Master. Like Saul, Peter came to see who Jesus was – the Messiah, Son of the living God – although it took him much longer to reconcile himself to seeing him as the Suffering Servant, a theme which later became so prevalent in his first letter. Like Saul, he was blown away by the resurrection of Christ: 'Praise be to the God and Father of our Lord Jesus Christ! . . . he has given us new birth into a living hope through the resurrection of Jesus Christ from the dead' (1 Peter 1:3). And he made a firm and final decision to follow Jesus, even though he knew it would lead to his death (John 21). His subsequent life, graphically described in Acts as he starts to lead the new movement so courageously, is as impressive as that of Saul the rabbi who became Paul the apostle.

Perhaps this is the New Testament's way of telling us that those four elements – of need, understanding something of Jesus, his death and resurrection, the costly decision to follow him, and the evidence of a changed life – are standing requirements in any who claim to be Christians. It is not a question of emotion. That may or may not be present. It is a matter of the will. It is not a question of suddenness – Peter's path was long and drawn out. It is not a matter of just talking the talk, but of walking the walk. God, who is so flexible in the way he approaches us and calls us to his service, makes it very clear that true Christianity always involves the humbling of human pride and the recognition of human need. It always requires the recognition of Jesus as divine as well as human, and sees his death and resurrection as intrinsic to God's act of rescue. It always looks for a determination to follow Jesus, marked publicly by baptism. And without a manifest change of life, no claim to be a Christian can stand.

Chapter 3

FUMBLING FIRST EFFORTS

If you have a passion to share with others the discovery of the difference Jesus Christ makes to life, where do you begin? Well, it all depends, of course, on your circumstances. I was a boy in my mid teens in an English public school. And talking about Jesus Christ was most definitely not cool. It was entirely out of order. So I had to proceed with care. Looking back, I realize that I quickly tumbled, unwittingly, into one of the best ways of spreading the gospel. Invitation.

Invitation
I had accepted the invitation of Richard Gorrie to the Christian house party that he had found so helpful. I went, not knowing quite what to expect. It was still wartime, and we worked on the land during the mornings, enjoyed a wide variety of games in the afternoons, and lively worship and high-quality talks on the Christian life in the evenings. I had never experienced anything like it. The large house party of 150 or so was split

down into small dormitories, where we slept and soon
developed close friendships with others. Some of these friendships continue to this day. I found the whole thing an enormous
help. I enjoyed the friendships, the sport, the talks and the
discussions. I realized that it was all expressly designed to
introduce boys like me to a living faith in Christ, and although
I had committed myself shortly before going there, I saw what
a good evangelistic agency this was. It was more or less impossible to speak about Jesus to my friends at school – it was
simply not done, and in any case, I did not know enough. But
I could invite them to this house party, which took place three
times a year. A number of my friends came, and most of them
became enthusiastic Christians.

In those far-off days, schools such as mine still had the
practice of 'fagging', where a senior boy would have the help
of two or three 'fags' to do simple tasks for him. It was a
practice that could easily be abused, but I liked my fags and
invited several of them to the house party. It was a very effective
way of evangelism, and most of them became committed
Christians. Indeed, I went into National Service on the same
day as one of them. We had adjoining beds in the barrack
room. And we both got on our knees to try to pray on the first
night – more aware of Radio Luxembourg and the noise in
the barrack room than we were of God. Still, it raised the flag,
and immediately next morning someone in the room came to
ask my advice about trouble in his marriage. 'Wife trouble?' I
asked. 'I haven't even got a wife yet.' But it started a useful
conversation.

Ever since those early days at school, I have been convinced
of the importance of invitation. It is the 'Come and see'

approach which we find more than once in the first chapter of St John's Gospel. It does not preach. It does not tell someone else what to do. Both are very objectionable in today's society. But it is warm, allows the other person an easy way out if he or she is so disposed, and is collegial: not 'Go on your own' but 'Why not come with me?' Statistics in the US show that over 70% of the population would accept, if invited to church by someone they liked. In Britain the results would be much lower, but invitation remains a very effective method. That is how Christian groups in the universities grow – members invite their friends. And people come, not necessarily because they are interested in Christianity – they simply don't want to disappoint their friends. I wonder how many people we fail to reach, for the simple reason that we do not invite them? What are we afraid of? The worst they can do is to refuse.

Conversation
I recall Billy Graham speaking to us theological students at Cambridge University on one of his visits to Britain. There was considerable scepticism in those days about his methods, particularly about the mass evangelism that is associated with his name. But he said something like this: 'Mass evangelism is not the best way to spread the gospel, but it is the way God has entrusted to me. The best way is when there is one person who has good news to share, and one who is keen to hear it.' It was very interesting to receive this commendation of personal evangelism from one whose gifting lay so strongly in another direction.

I started to attempt this one-to-one way of spreading the gospel while I was a senior boy at school. My friend, who was later head boy, captained the school in cricket and rugby, and won a scholarship to Cambridge, was interested in what had gripped me. So we had long talks about it, mostly when we were in adjoining beds as prefects in a dormitory whose boys had long since gone to sleep. At times, he was so challenged by Christ that he was visibly ill at ease as he wrestled with whether or not to give in to Christ. Well, he did not. But many years later he got in touch with me again out of the blue. He had gone into the Colonial Service after university and was a District Officer in Kenya. There he was profoundly impressed by the behaviour of the African Christians, and it was this which finally led him to that commitment which he had not made all those years ago. Interestingly, I was at that time Principal of St John's Theological College, Nottingham, training men for ordination. His conversion was so profound that he felt he should offer for ordination, and he even came and spent a term or so in the college. But Christ was calling him to himself, not to ordination, and he became an outstanding leader in a Christian charity instead.

Although I was not immediately successful, I realized that this personal approach to a friend was an invaluable way of spreading the gospel. For one thing it was private, and nobody was tempted to play to the gallery. For another, it enabled the two of us to get alongside each other and see what the Bible had to say. It enabled the Christian partner in the conversation to try to meet some of the objections and misunderstandings that were raised. And, as I discovered later, it gave the chance for the other person to pray quietly and commit his life to Christ as we talked these things over. It turned me into a lifelong advocate of this one-to-one ministry.

After Oxford I found myself as a National Serviceman in the Royal Artillery. Basic training was very demanding. The NCOs were often sadistic, and many men had a miserable time. As I had been to university first, I was a bit older than most, and had the opportunity of helping one or two of the soldiers in my barrack room to faith. I found that they respected someone who was decisive about his Christianity, and whose manner of life and language was consistent. Foul language was so normal in the army that, if someone did not use it, they immediately stood out, and this gave a good opportunity to explain one's faith. I remember one evening when I had been to a very low-grade late supper in the canteen – which only the hungriest used to frequent. When I got back, I found that the men in the barrack room had gathered round and wanted me to explain what it meant to be a Christian. This was a wonderful occasion, and I saw how a mixture of lifestyle and one-to-one conversations could open up the way for speaking to a larger group.

Actually that happened at the end of the first week of basic training, when we were allowed out to the nearby town for the first time, with strict instructions on how to avoid catching sexually transmitted diseases! I discovered a detachment of the Salvation Army playing their instruments in the town, but nobody seemed to be speaking. So I went up and asked them if it would not be a good idea to say something about the gospel to the people gathered around, the very motivation that originally drove the Salvation Army on to the streets. This was, I suppose, my first venture into open-air preaching, though it was short and conversational. It was a reminder to me that, although Christian presence and Christian lifestyle are vital, it was also important to engage in Christian proclamation, or else nobody would really know what makes us tick.

Proclamation

I don't think I ever needed to be persuaded that the good news of Christ needed to be passed on to other people, however oblivious to it they seemed to be. It was the best news in the world – that there is a living God, that he wants to communicate with us, that he has sent his Son to reveal him and to die for us, and that he longs to have us living in close contact with him. Obviously, therefore, those who had discovered this gospel needed to pass it on. In addition to the ways which I have just outlined, it was clear to me that I needed to acquire skill in commending this gospel verbally, in an organized and attractive way, especially if I was going to be ordained. Having been exposed to so many bad sermons, I did not want to add unnecessarily to their number.

I was very fortunate, because at the Christian house party, to which I referred above, there was very careful training of young speakers. From them I learned the need for a clear aim, biblical content, a structure that everyone could follow, a natural manner, good illustrations, and a well-organized beginning and conclusion to the address. I had given a few talks at this house party, and again at the Christian Union meeting in school, but I was very much a beginner. I can still recall my very first talk, to boys in the school Christian Union. Someone passed by the French window as I was speaking, and looked in. I totally lost it. I was stopped dead in my tracks. I did not know where I was in my talk's plan, nor where I was hoping to go next. It was a disaster! This incident really shook me, and it took me some time to recover. But I learnt a useful lesson from it. If you are speaking in a smallish gathering and are shy about eye contact, look just over the head of the people in the back row, and everyone will feel that you are looking at them and speaking to them. I do not do that now. I like to watch faces to see the impact of what is being said. But I was very grateful for that tip in the early days.

I did a small amount of preaching in the army, particularly to a Brethren Assembly which, though pacifist in tendency, still liked to have an officer in uniform preaching occasionally! But then came the real test. It stands out vividly in my memory. I was asked to do a weekend of ministry for the Christian Union in Oxford, which at that time was over 300 strong.

A weekend's ministry included giving a Bible exposition on the Saturday night and an evangelistic sermon on the Sunday night. It was the Sunday night that terrified me. How could a sheer beginner like me preach evangelistically to those who were only three or four years younger than myself? So I was relieved when I discovered that the dates were for the ninth weekend of the Oxford summer term, when most of the students would already have left. An ideal place to try out a beginner! What relieved me even more was that I could not manage the date! I thought and rather hoped that this would settle the matter, but no. They wrote back and asked me for a date in the middle of the spring term, but once again I could not manage it. To my complete amazement, they came back with an invitation for the third weekend of the autumn term, the time when all the fresher students were new and seeking to find a basis for their university life and friendships. The date was free, and I knew I had to accept.

There were two things that made the project even more forbidding. One was that they demanded that I should preach on human sin from Romans 3. The other was that in those days there was a church at the end of Turl Street in the heart of Oxford, which the Christian Union used every Sunday night during term. It is now the library of the adjoining Lincoln College. At all events, one of the notable features of this church was an enormous high pulpit, reached by a staircase with a door at the top to shut you in! As if that was not bad enough, when the preacher began, the lights were turned out. Such was my initiation into university evangelism!

It was customary to pray with the members of the committee in the vestry beforehand, and I know that I prayed with great fervour and a lot of trepidation that night. I remember it vividly. At the end, I knew I would need to make an appeal for those who wanted to take things further to come to the front seats for a short talk on the way to faith in Christ. This did not happen every week, but it was customary in the first few weeks of the autumn term when many students, especially freshers, were weighing up their options. I made the appeal, though with no great sense of conviction. Imagine my surprise, then, when I found that a dozen or more came to the front and asked how they could find this faith in Christ. Most of them seem to have come to the Lord that night, and of course I was mightily relieved and utterly overjoyed. Often since then I have had no response to an evangelistic challenge. That does not bother me. I know that God has his time and his way of approaching people. As long as I have been faithful in making the gospel plain, I can leave the results to him. But I needed to see results on that first night! And God in his goodness gave them.

FUMBLING FIRST EFFORTS   49

Several lessons impressed themselves on me from that incident. First, the fact that, if God wants you to do something or go somewhere, then he has a way of getting through to you! He certainly got through to me. It was almost unheard of for a complete beginner to be let loose in a prestigious university sermon as early as the third week of the new academic year, when, if he messed it up, this could seriously damage the work for the rest of the year. I think I began to learn then that most of all God needs his people to be flexible and adaptable and to listen to his call, even if it seems improbable. I am sure Philip the evangelist, of whom we read in Acts 8, had learned that lesson well. He was the preacher at an unprecedented revival in Samaria, and God called him to leave it all and go into the desert 70 miles away, without knowing if he would meet anyone at all there. We read that Philip got up and went. Often we are so immersed in the here and now, so wedded to our regular way of doing things, that we are deaf when the divine whisper comes our way, telling us that he wants us to attempt something new.

The second thing I learned on that occasion was the paramount need for prayer. God was the evangelist, not me. So I needed to cast myself wholly on him for his words, his encouragement and his peace. I am not sure that I fulfilled those conditions, but I did pray, earnestly and repeatedly. I think I realized even in those early days that only God could bring someone 'from darkness to light, and from the power of Satan to God', as the New Testament tellingly puts it (Acts 26:18). That was something I could not do. So I needed to cry to the Lord to open blind eyes, to touch hard hearts and strengthen volatile wills. Nothing in evangelism happens without prayer.

The third thing I recall from this incident was the great care I gave to preparation – propelled by dread! I needed a clear structure, I needed to be faithful to the text, and I needed effective illustrations and a clear concluding challenge. Care in preparation is as necessary as prayer. Prayer points to God's part in the enterprise, care to ours. There is no excuse for sloppy preparation, or hoping that something will come on the spur of the moment.

The final lesson I began to learn from all of this was the need to make a decisive challenge to follow Christ. That was very alien to the civilized Anglican tradition which had been my background. It was thought rather daring even to end a sermon with a prayer in those far-off days! But how could I avoid making a challenge? After all, that is what the apostles did time and again, as the record stands in Acts. In so doing, they were merely following the example of their Lord who had called people decisively into discipleship. That word 'discipleship' is so important. No evangelist worth his or her salt is after a mere decision. That can be emotionally stimulated, a flash in the pan. What the evangelist is seeking is a change of allegiance, a change of lifestyle, a change of direction for the subsequent life. Authentic decision leads to discipleship. And discipleship starts when the hearers thoughtfully entrust their lives to Christ and say, 'Yes, I do want to follow you, and I want to make a start on it tonight.'

Those four lessons have stayed with me in evangelistic preaching from that day to this. I am grateful that, in the goodness of God, I did not have to wait half a lifetime to discover them.

Chapter 4

WHAT GOOD NEWS?

So far this book has inevitably had something of an auto-biographical flavour. From now on, while not excluding personal reflections, it will become more thematic.

The Christian faith has been around a long time. It has grown into the largest belief system the world has ever known. One of the first names attached to its message was 'good news', the Greek *euaggelion*, from which we derive the word 'evangelism'. Over the centuries it has been accommodated to countless cultures. It has fragmented into endless denominations. It is beset with a great many distortions, confusions and misunderstandings.

Many people believe that the Christianity they find in the churches is not good news. It is neither good nor news. Not news, because they think they have heard it all before. It is about God, who seems unknown and far away, if he exists at all. It is about a baby Jesus in a manger or a dead Jesus on a cross. That is not very appealing or life enhancing. Frankly, it is not news.

Moreover, it is not particularly good. The professed followers of Jesus seem no improvement on anyone else. They are prone to fall out with one another. Many of them seem to be hypocrites. They are often dull: their Christianity seems to drain all the joy out of life. Their marriages do not stand up any better than other people's. They are, on the whole, not more friendly, more ready to help, than those who make no Christian profession at all. That is how it seems to a lot of people these days, and, in the UK at least, this is the third generation of those who have felt that way, and consequently have nothing to do with the church.

Arguably these people have never been exposed to the real article, and they are rightly fed up with the various imitations. Anyone who sets out to evangelize, to bring the truly good news to such people, needs to give a lot of thought as to how it can become fresh for them, real news, and how it can be seen to be the wonderfully good thing it is.

Some years ago I wrote a book about the resurrection. It fell into the hands of a woman who wrote to me in excitement: 'I always thought Christianity and church were about forgiveness of sins, and that did not excite me much. But now I realize it is something much, much more. It is relationship with Jesus, who broke the power of death and is alive for ever. I am nearly fifty years old, and have often been in church, but I have never realized this until your book came my way. This is the message that should be shouted from churches every Sunday.' Suddenly Christianity had become news for that woman, and good news at that.

Only today I have had this letter from a twenty-three-year-old Bulgarian graduate, leading a Christian team in Oxford

that is reaching out to the overseas students, many of them
Muslim, who crowd into the city in July and August. Towards
the end of two weeks, when the Christian team have been
befriending visitors in the street, taking them to a café, and
inviting them, if they wish, to a Bible study, this is what he
writes to me: 'We welcomed a brother from Iran who came to
Christ last night. So did a Chinese man and a Palestinian girl.
Pray that they may sense the Spirit of God working in their
lives. The Bible studies have been amazing. Students from
Saudi Arabia, the Emirates, Libya, Syria and many other
countries have come to them, and are really excited to learn
more and hear the gospel. The other day some of our team did
dramas in the Cornmarket [the main pedestrian street in the
city], and last night I preached on the love of God, and we had
many wonderful talks with the people afterwards. This outreach
has been amazing.'

I can share his enthusiasm. Authentic Christianity *is*
amazing. However, not all that passes for Christianity is the
authentic article.

Inadequate understandings of the good news
It might be worth glancing at some of the inadequate present-
ations of the good news, that either confuse or mislead. Dr
William Abraham has very helpfully looked at four of them
in his book, *The Art of Evangelism*.[1]

Some people imagine that the heart of the good news is that
Jesus came to this world in order to bring us self-esteem and
peace of mind. The focus here is on the brokenness, loneliness
and frustration of many people, whereas God wants to give us
contentment and peace of mind. Conversion for such people

means coming to respect ourselves, accept God's love for us, and pass it on to other people.

Others, particularly in some parts of the evangelical tradition, see Jesus as the one who came to this earth only in order to save us from hell and damnation. And the good news, through this interpretation, is that God, the Judge, has sent Jesus, the Saviour, to bear the punishment we deserve. Unless we accept this good news, we shall be lost for ever. Conversion means turning to Christ in order to secure a place in heaven when we die.

A third scenario sees Jesus as the one who came to liberate humankind from bondage and oppression. This may be from dictatorship, poverty, racism, sexism, or anything else that holds people in bondage. Conversion, in this view, is seen as turning to a life which mirrors God's act of liberation in the exodus, and seeks to change the structures of society accordingly. This was the view that lay behind liberation theology, particularly, but not exclusively, in Latin America. If the previous view was vertical, saving people from this world, this approach is very horizontal, concentrating almost exclusively on salvation in this present world.

The fourth view Abraham writes about is the notion that Jesus came to bring us health and wealth. The key conviction here is that God is good and wants us to prosper. If we are not prospering financially or in health, something is wrong. The good news is that this can all be put right. We can prosper and enjoy perfect health, if we turn to Christ and give generously to the ministry of those who brought this good news to us. Giving is an 'investment' to gain further riches and blessing from God.

It would not be difficult to add further misrepresentations of the gospel to Abraham's list. For many, Christianity is a matter of not doing anybody any harm (what a negative idea!) or being a good neighbour (you don't need Jesus for that). But all of these misunderstandings of the gospel fall under the central stricture which Abraham brings against them. The good news is made to place an emphasis on ourselves and what we need: to be affirmed, to be rescued from hell, to be liberated or to be healed. It all focuses not on God, but on us and our needs. It is pure selfishness. Christ is merely a means to the end of our satisfaction in all these various schemes. And that makes the gospel hopelessly narrow. It has no room for what God has done in creation, or in human history. It says nothing about the church, or the future God has for the world.

So Abraham puts forward several elements which must be included in any balanced understanding of the gospel. They are beliefs about creation, the uniqueness of human beings, a diagnosis of what is wrong with the world, clarity about the solution, a vision for the future, a way of living, and, he might well have added, a community that embodies the good news. He concludes that all we have to offer is Jesus Christ. John Wesley loved to write in his journal: 'I offered them Christ.'

Abraham concludes with three main convictions. First, the gospel is about God's action, not about ourselves or our moral maxims, utopian hopes, experiences or happiness. Secondly, the gospel is astonishing and unique. It is not a speculative philosophy, and does not consist in esoteric secrets about health and wealth, nor is it a recipe for middle-class decent living. It is essentially a narrative about Jesus Christ, his person, his cross and resurrection. And thirdly, he is convinced that the gospel is intrinsically attractive. The Christian evangelist has no need to apologize for it, still less attempt to improve on it. There can be nothing greater than God's involvement in history to save the world. Lose that emphasis, and you retreat to one of these inadequate expressions of the good news. But when people taste the authentic article, they will sell all that they have to get more.

I have a great respect for Dr Abraham, not only because he is an orthodox and highly intelligent academic, but because he is a practitioner in evangelism as well. Not every author on evangelism is to be found, as Abraham is, going into prisons with the good news of Christ.

I myself would try to sum up the heart of the gospel in five statements – all good, and all news.

A correct understanding – the heart of the Christian good news

First, we believe in God

Christians believe that we are not cosmic orphans, and this world is not a random fluke, governed by chance. It shows all the marks of intelligent design. By whatever evolutionary development the world reached its present state, Christians want to maintain that it has a Creator who originated it and now sustains it, a Creator who is involved in the existence of every person, every tree, every sunset. Though far transcending this world, God is intimately involved in it, like an artist with his painting, a composer with his music. That is why a concern for the environment is important in the proclamation of the gospel in our generation. Older people may be casual about it, but the young are not. They are passionate to conserve a world which is rapidly being ravaged by human beings. And their concern is a profoundly biblical one. We are given by God the task of being stewards and overseers of his created order. Two other convictions about God are central in Christian belief. One is that God is utterly just and holy, and the other is that he loves and cares intensely for the people he has made.

Of course, this view is strongly contested by an increasingly articulate 'New Atheism', which is advanced both in serious academic books and by more popular writers such as Richard Dawkins in *The God Delusion* and Christopher Hitchens in *God is Not Great*. They have not come up with new arguments against the existence of God. But they have advanced the old arguments in a fresh and confident, not to say strident, tone, which has gone down well in the increasingly secular society in which we live. There is good reason to believe in God, but this is not the place to consider those arguments. We shall do so in a later chapter on the importance of apologetics. Our purpose here is to state the essential nature of the God Christians believe in – a holy, loving Creator and sustainer of the entire universe.

Secondly, we believe that God is not silent

God is not unknowable, nor is he indifferent to his creation and deaf to our cries. The universe is not silent. God has revealed himself in many ways. The natural world is part of his self-disclosure. As the psalmist put it,

> The heavens declare the glory of God;
> the skies proclaim the work of his hands . . .

There is no speech or language
   where their voice is not heard.
Their voice goes out into all the earth,
   their words to the ends of the world.
(Psalm 19:1–4)

A colleague of mine who has just cycled from Land's End to John O'Groats writes, 'We saw some stunning parts of the British Isles, helped by the vista from the saddle, the rural routes and lovely cycle tracks. God's creation is truly marvellous. I found myself musing, "Who does Richard Dawkins praise when he sees the beauty of the natural world?"'

God has not only revealed himself in the natural world, but in human personality at its best. Whenever we meet love, generosity, beauty, truthfulness, goodness and self-sacrifice in the life of another human being, be he or she Christian or not, there is a reflection of what God is like. Of course the reflection is far from perfect. There is just one perfect reflection, in the life and character of Jesus Christ. All human virtues fall short of that. Nevertheless, the sheer goodness that we often meet in other people is a pointer to the God who is perfection.

Another way in which God has revealed something of himself is in the course of history. There have been more than twenty civilizations in the course of recorded history, and they follow a remarkable pattern. Each one arises from obscurity or slavery, experiences a rise to significance, followed by a flowering of the civilization, before its corruption and degeneration, leading to the decline and eventual slavery from which it originally emerged. It seems as if God will not tolerate overweening pride and arrogance in any human institution. They all have within them the seeds of their destruction. There is an ethical dimension in the course of history, and it is one of the ways in which God shows his hand.

The most fascinating history of all is the story of Israel. Originating with a desert sheikh and his family some four thousand years ago, the Jewish people have had no geographical home for nearly half of that period. And yet they have remained recognizably a nation group, with facial and cultural features intact, and now many of them have returned to the land from which they were ruthlessly ejected in AD 135. There is no other nation in the world that has survived hardships comparable to those of the Jews. It is hard to doubt that there is something special about this people. And Scripture tells us that indeed there is. This is the people through whom, for all their failures, God intended to show the rest of the world something of his nature and his standards.

The greatest Jew who ever lived was undeniably Jesus of Nazareth. Those who knew him best were convinced that in him 'all the fulness of the Deity lives in bodily form' (Colossians 2:9). They were sure that God, who had revealed himself in many different ways down through the centuries, had spoken decisively and finally in one who shared his nature as well as ours. And that is unique among the religions of the world. In Islam, for example, another great monotheistic faith, Allah is distant. He remains unknowable, despite the ninety-nine descriptive names accorded him. He never reveals himself. He only reveals his will, and to that will the only proper response is *islam*, 'submission'. How different from the God revealed in the Bible! That book is all about the God who refuses to hide himself. It is about revelation. And on the basis of that revelation the carriers of the good news have something solid to pass on to others. It is not human speculation about the divine. It is what God has shown us about himself.

Thirdly, we believe in a God who rescues

Scripture and experience join in maintaining that all is not well with humankind. You only have to turn on the TV for the evening news to be convinced of that. Our thoughts, our words, our actions, our inclinations, our characters are all infected with the 'human disease' of self-centredness, of 'sin' as the Bible calls it. It is very dangerous, this disease. In fact it is lethal. Try as we may, there is nothing we can do to rescue ourselves from its clutches. As with AIDS, there is no lasting cure. Religious devotions and moral behaviour are both admirable, but they are inadequate. They cannot get us to God, nor can they make us fit to be seen in his holy presence. Still less can they neutralize the virus of sin in our lives.

But the amazing testimony of the whole Bible is that God has stepped in, through Jesus Christ who shares our human nature, to do for us what we could never do for ourselves. If we look hard enough at the evidence presented to us in the Scriptures penned by Jesus' contemporaries, we will see that 'God was reconciling the world to himself in Christ' (2 Corinthians 5:19). And the cross was where it happened. That cross was not the sad end of a great life. It was not that the Mafia eventually caught up with Jesus. And it was not just to show us how much God loves us. No, the cross was the place where God once and for all took personal responsibility for the sins of the entire world. He burdened himself with them. They crushed him. But that was not the end of the story. Death was not the final victor over the Lord of life. Jesus was raised from the grave on the first Easter Day by the Father's power, and he now offers the Holy Spirit of God to those who will turn to him and humbly ask for it. Think of it – a clean slate for all your past, and the Lord's own power to remake you for the future. And at the end of the day, a life to be shared with him beyond death, of which his resurrection is the guarantee and pledge. Good news indeed! I have seen it transform the lives of prostitutes and politicians alike. It is not dull and churchy. It is the most important message in the world. This story of 'God to the rescue' is not only the actual meaning of the name 'Jesus'; it is one of the central themes of the whole Bible. The God who reveals himself to humankind is the same God who rescues humankind. He is the God who can with perfect justice acquit the ungodly because he has himself shouldered our debts and drunk the poison of our sins to the very last dregs. Where can you find anything remotely comparable in all the religions of the world?

Fourthly, we believe in a God who gives new life

The Holy Spirit is that part of the Triune God who is available to come and inhabit the lives of those who will accept him. And when that happens, it makes all the difference. We no longer have to struggle on, rowing against the currents of life. We are able to erect our sail, so to speak, and find the wind of the Spirit propelling us along. The Holy Spirit is not to be confused with our own spirit. The difference is very marked in Hebrew, where *nephesh* is the word normally used for our human spirit, the life force that sets us apart from a corpse or a tailor's dummy. But *ruach* is the word regularly used for God's Spirit, which he offers to impart. It is a powerful word and suggests a gale, an invasion. It is no less than the Spirit of Jesus which he promised his followers would receive. And when that Spirit is welcomed into one's life, things do not remain as they were before. There is a new understanding of spiritual truth, a new freedom in prayer, a new sense of belonging to Christ and his people, a new power over bad habits, a new desire to tell others, a new delight in Christian fellowship, a new humility, boldness and desire to learn. Those are the results, gradually and variously evidenced, of the 'new birth', which God brings about in those who 'convert' or turn to him in repentance and faith, and are sealed with the sacrament of baptism into his church.

And when an individual welcomes that Spirit into his or her life, they find they have become part of a family, the Christian community or church – for the Spirit not only enlivens the individual, but creates the church, which is sometimes in the New Testament seen as the temple which the Spirit inhabits. This Christian family stretches down the centuries and across the world. It embraces people of every nation and language. Their purpose in life is to live their lives for the credit of the Lord who has rescued them. Believers become part of Christ's body on earth, enlivened by his Spirit. And when this life is over, God will welcome them to his eternal home. That's the deal!

Finally, we believe in a God who sends
All through Scripture and throughout history, people who have found – or rather, been found by – this living, Triune,

redemptive God have something to declare. They cannot keep quiet. They speak because they must. They have found treasure, and they want others to share it. The Lord loves them and gave himself for them. The least they can do is to seek with all their power to introduce others to him. That is the motive that lies at the heart of all evangelism. God asks, 'Whom shall I send, and who will go for us?' And the evangelist replies, humbly but with love and wholeheartedness, 'Lord, here am I: send me.' I think of the owner of one of the major businesses in the UK, one of the All Blacks rugby forwards, a government minister, a previous captain of the Australian cricket team. None of them could keep quiet about Jesus, once they had discovered him. They were compelled by the sheer joy of it to tell others.

The good news of the gospel contains a lot more than that. But I suggest that those five propositions lie very near its centre.

A correct understanding – the relevance of the good news
This Christian good news connects with so many of the situations in which ordinary people find themselves.

A great many people are *lonely*. You see it on the school desk with a question scratched on it: 'Why am I so lonely when all these people are here?' You see it in the growing proportion of single-occupancy houses. You see it in the way many cannot face silence or being on their own. And while there is no panacea for this, the good news offers very substantial help, through the presence of the Lord in the very lives of his followers, once they come to him, and his promise: 'I will never leave you nor forsake you' (Joshua 1:5). I recall an old woman living on her own in a derelict farmhouse. I had the privilege of leading her to Christ, and although she often fell on the floor and was unable to get up, she told me what a comfort it was to have the presence of the Lord with her.

Lots of folk feel *empty* inside, including, very often, some of the big achievers. The psychologist Jung once observed, 'The central neurosis of our lives is loneliness.' Jack Higgins, author of the celebrated novel *The Eagle Has Landed*, among a crop of best-sellers, commented, 'I'm glad that I did not know at eighteen that when you get to the top there is only emptiness.' The good news is that there is a cure for emptiness. Jesus said, 'I have come that they may have life, and have it to the full' (John 10:10), and countless people have proved that to be true, whatever their nationality or state in society. Only the other day I was listening to a famous ex-model who had everything: celebrity, riches, beauty, world acclaim. But she felt empty inside. She despised the shallowness of the glittering crowd around her, and she tried various avenues to find satisfaction. All in vain, until she found Jesus Christ, and for many years now her life has shown the joy and fulfilment which so long had eluded her.

Others are tortured by *guilt*. They have done something in the past that haunts them. They cannot get rid of it, try as they may. Often people distress themselves by feeling guilty about something for which they are not responsible: that is false guilt. But there is such a thing as real guilt, being in the wrong with God. The good news, as we've seen already, is that Christ took personal responsibility for our guilt and 'therefore, there is now no condemnation for those who are in Christ Jesus' (Romans 8:1). I have seen murderers come to an assurance of forgiveness and a new start in life, once they realized that Another had borne their guilt. Indeed, I remember once sitting next to a sniper who had shot many people, including women and children, and was tortured by the memories. I had the joy of pointing him to Jesus. He was overwhelmed to realize that he was accepted because of what Christ had done, although in himself he was totally unacceptable. And his relief and gratitude were a privilege to behold.

Yet others are enslaved by *bad habits* which they cannot break. These may involve drugs, alcohol or pornography. Or they may be more acceptable but equally enslaving habits such as greed, laziness or constant criticism of others. But the testimony of the New Testament and of contemporary experience is that the indwelling Christ can break those fetters which spoil our lives, and that the very power which raised him from the dead is available to rescue us from the living death of a bondage from which we felt we could never escape. A winsome example is a man such as Tom Tarrants, once full of hatred for black people and an active member of the Ku Klux Klan, but now a mature Christian and the Director of the C. S. Lewis Institute in Washington DC. You would find him the most gentle, gracious man you could imagine, much sought after for his wise spiritual counsel.

Or reflect on the *alienation* which runs through contemporary society, alienation within the family, in the workplace or between groups and between countries. The world is full of it. But the good news is that there is hope for the alienated. Christ died to reconcile two classically alienated parties, Jews and Gentiles, to himself and hence to each other (cf. Ephesians 2:12–22), and he has been doing this ever since. In a mission in Zimbabwe, I recall several divorced couples coming together in a renewed marriage, after both partners had come to faith. I recall a murderer and the wife of the man he murdered doing a tour throughout Britain to show reconciliation, after both had come to Christ. Jesus can banish the alienation which no medicine on earth can touch.

Yes, there is indeed good news. Christians have been entrusted with it. And it is highly relevant to every nation and individual in our world. Jesus is the good news in person. Let's make a better fist of passing it on!

Chapter 5

CHURCH ALIVE

We're all in this together

Perhaps it is the effect of Western individualism, perhaps the perceived ineffectiveness of the church as an institution, but I notice nowadays a growing tendency for Christians to go it alone and neglect the fellowship of other believers. Some of them have given up entirely on church. But community is vitally important if we are to make any impact on society. It simply will not do to have our Christian faith privatized into a personal creed. Nor will the gospel spread very far that way.

Community is also important to counteract the 'aloneness' felt by many modern people. They may live and work in a crowd, they may fill their lives with excitements, but deep down they sense an isolation, a loneliness to which the Christian gospel and the people who commend it are at least a partial solution. Everybody needs community.

There is not only an evangelistic and a sociological basis, but also a strong theological basis for community. God has revealed himself in the Scriptures *as community*. The Father, the Son and the Holy Spirit exist together in the Godhead. To become a Christian is essentially to take a stake in the God who is community. Have you seen that famous icon which portrays the Father, the Son and the Spirit gathered round a table laden with good food, and the other side of the table is open, waiting for you and me? Evangelism is drawing someone into the family of the Triune God. So going it alone is not an acceptable option. Christianity which does not begin with the individual does not begin. But Christianity which ends with the individual, ends.

And if theological reflection does not move us, perhaps there is a very obvious practical point that will. Christians working together in community demonstrate good news, and do not merely talk about it. Together we can achieve far more than any of us could individually. The interaction of members with different skills is attractive. The partnership and camaraderie, the sheer mutual support, are things we all need. And when unity and coherence are directed outwards for the good of those who are not members, they are winsome and real. (That is the true meaning of the Catholic tag, *extra ecclesiam nulla salus*: 'outside the church there is no salvation', words easily misunderstood, but properly drawing attention to the new community formed by the God who rescues each one of us individually.) That is one reason why I rarely engage in evangelism on my own: I go as one of a team. It is so much more attractive and effective.

The impact of Christian community
In Acts 11 we are given a graphic description of the impact caused, not by individuals, but by a Christian community or

task force engaged in evangelizing Antioch, the capital of Syria. This was no five-year plan, no top apostle that won Antioch for the gospel, but God and a bunch of homeless refugees. We do not know the name of a single one of them, but they formed a counterculture which became the springboard for evangelism, not only in that city but in the ensuing Gentile mission.

It is worth focusing on their characteristics, because these point the way to what a church alive for mission could look like in our own day. I've listed twelve.

1. They were first and foremost **a lay initiative** (see Acts 11:19; cf. 8:1–5). There was not a single official 'minister' among them. Like the Universities and Colleges Christian Fellowship (UCCF), Agape, Youth for Christ and the London City Mission, theirs was a lay initiative. Evangelism under passionate lay leadership is often the most effective.

2. These early missionaries had learned how to **sacrifice** (11:19). They had been kicked out of Jerusalem as dangerous disturbers of religious peace. They had lost jobs, homes and families. They were constantly on the move. They did not know where they would lay their heads each night or where their next meal would come from. It is Christians who, like their Master, have learned to sacrifice, that make the greatest impact.

3. These missionaries were Hellenists (Jews who spoke Greek and often behaved like Greeks). They were **not bound by past** Jewish **customs**. They were followers of Stephen (11:19; 8:1–4). And he was stoned to death for his views! In Acts 6:11–14 we find that he dared to assert that God does not live in buildings, that he is not exclusively encountered through a book, and that he is not bound by the customs derived from

the past. No wonder they killed him! If you were to maintain today that God is not to be found in a building, a holy book or what we did last year, you might not get stoned, but you would get a distinctly frosty reception in most churches!

4. These men were **enthusiasts**. They could not keep quiet about Jesus (11:20). They had previously been preaching him only to the Jews, but in this great Greek city they saw that Jesus was for everyone: they spoke 'to Greeks also, telling them the good news about the Lord Jesus'. That short phrase of two words, 'Lord Jesus', is all we are told about their message. But 'Jesus' means 'God to the rescue', and 'Lord' asserts his supremacy over every other being. Not a bad summary of the news they were so passionate about. But today, do you find that same passion, centring on Jesus? Not often. You could go into many a church and hear nothing passionate, least of all enthusiastic, about Jesus. You could listen to many editions of the three-minute *Thought for the Day* on the BBC, often delivered by eminent church leaders, but scarcely ever hear the name of Jesus! Lack of enthusiasm makes Christianity, the most exciting news in the world, seem boring.

5. These early missionaries were not satisfied with a simple challenge to respond to Jesus. They majored on **teaching**. First Barnabas, and then Barnabas and Saul, spent an entire year meeting with the church and teaching a great many people (11:26). No hit-and-run evangelism here, but challenge backed up by effective and sustained teaching. You rarely find that combination in today's churches, but when you do, that church grows.

6. But teaching alone is not enough. There has to be **real love** bubbling up in the congregation. At Antioch there was.

Believers of Jewish and Gentile origin so enjoyed one another's fellowship that they actually ate together – something unheard of. When Barnabas arrived, sent by the Jerusalem church to see what was going on, he could only describe it as 'the grace of God' (11:23) to find such warm cross-cultural fellowship. I recall one Sunday asking people in our church to declare their nationality, and I think there were fourteen nationalities altogether, with various colours of skin. No wonder nobody wanted to leave when the services were over, but to stay, chat and pray.

7. This Antioch church did not have a bishop, a priest or a minister. No, it operated with **shared leadership**. We are given the names of their leadership team of five in Acts 13:1. They came from a variety of countries and backgrounds. They had varied emphases, too. Some were teachers, rooted in the Scriptures. Others were 'prophets', or charismatics as we would call them today, relying on the Holy Spirit for inspiration. But this did not make them split up, as it would do in many of today's churches. They stayed together and drew on one another's strengths. Shared leadership is a great safeguard against both tyrannical leadership and loneliness in leadership. In our Oxford church, we had quite a large leadership team: male and female, ordained and lay, graduate and non-graduate, charismatic and non-charismatic. This was one of the reasons why the church grew. We need more of it today, when so many churches suffer from boredom under one-person leadership.

8. There was among them none of that false separation between a spiritual gospel and a social gospel which has disfigured much recent Christianity. This highly spiritual church had a strong sense of **social responsibility**. Some members

may have been among the Hellenistic Christians who fed
the impoverished widows, whom we read about in Acts 6.
Moreover, they did not, as we might be tempted to do, simply
throw money at the problem: they put a human face on their
gift by sending it via Barnabas and Saul (11:27ff.). The church
that cares for the poor will never lack respect – or adherents.
Perhaps that is why the Salvation Army and the Church Army
win such respect. They hold together a spiritual gospel, along
with social concern and service.

9. Most people seeking a church are drawn by its **worship**.
The worship at Antioch is instructive, and the word used (13:2)
is the one from which we derive 'liturgy'. This certainly did
not mean reading it all out of a book, but it did indicate
freedom within a recognized framework, and that is still the
most attractive worship. The people practised fasting, and self-
denial is an essential Christian virtue. They were not tied into
a prearranged worship programme, but were open to the inter-
vention of the Holy Spirit, no doubt through someone with
a prophetic gift. Presumably this word from God came in a
time of silent waiting on him. Silence is an important, and
often neglected, ingredient in worship. The people were then
prepared for costly obedience. How many churches today
would be happy to send two of their major leaders on foreign
mission, in response to a prophetic utterance? Personally, I
would be happy to share in the dynamic worship of a church
like that!

10. Clearly this Antioch church was passionate about
outreach. It was born through the mission of its refugees. But
it had not grown too settled, too respectable to continue to
care about, and try to reach, lost people and the regions beyond.

Thus it was prepared to obey the leading of the Spirit, and allow two of its most gifted ministers to go on mission, supporting them to the hilt. It is generally the case that the church which waters is itself watered.

11. In the account of the Antioch church (as in much of Acts), we notice a strong **emphasis on the Holy Spirit**. It is the Spirit who produces the attractive character of Barnabas (11:24), the Spirit who inspires the prophecy of Agabus (11:28), and the Spirit who designates (13:2) and then thrusts out that intrepid pair on the first missionary journey (13:4). Character, charisma, mission – happy the church which makes room for the Holy Spirit in all three areas.

12. Finally, this church seems to have made **Jesus top priority** in their life and organization. They were called 'Christians' for the first time here in Antioch. They did not take that name for themselves: they were 'disciples' or 'followers of the Way'. But other people called them Christians (11:26). They spoke of Christ. They served him. They tried to please him. Their way of life reminded people of Christ. And so the non-Christians called them 'Christians'. I wonder how many churches today would so remind the uncommitted of Jesus Christ that they would give them this nickname.

I have drawn these points from Luke's account of the church in Antioch, because the church was alive, not because it was perfect. And it was not. It hosted a major row between two apostles, which must have been very destructive to its life. But though not perfect, Antioch does embody some of the major markers of the sort of church God can use in evangelism, an illustration of the importance of a godly community in the furthering of the Christian message.

How can I motivate my church for evangelism?

Some drawbacks and hurdles
I have often been asked this question, especially by younger ministers. And it is not surprising. Today's church leaders have been raised in an increasingly secularist society. They are uncertain how to respond to the current postmodern worldview all around them. They have been brought up in churches that are concerned more with maintenance than with mission. After their theological training, they may themselves have lost their early confidence in the gospel and become unsure of what they believe. In any case that training was by books and essays, seminars and lectures. And their ministry involves none of these things, but real people! Teachers are trained partly in the schoolroom, doctors in clinical practice, engineers on the job. But not ministers. Consequently, emerging clergy often have very little experience of evangelism, and they probably harbour a fear of failure, perhaps even a fear of people. All of this causes them to be disinclined to bother about evangelism, when the path of church maintenance is easier and more respectable.

Sometimes there are additional reasons why ministers are so cautious about evangelism. They may have had a painful and unhappy first assignment under the leadership of someone older and supposedly wiser. Sometimes family strains claim too much of their attention. And many are frustrated with Victorian buildings which are utterly unsuited to modern needs and expectations, and yet the church cannot afford to replace them. Some clergy are terrified of offending wealthy members if they present the powerful challenge of the gospel as it appears in the New Testament. Some are discouraged by lack of fellowship, or by the conservative and unimaginative attitude of their congregation. Most are incompetent in the area of apologetics, being unable to sustain a convincing argument for their beliefs in the face of scepticism. Some get eaten up by wider ecclesiastical concerns. Many have little concern for the lost. I remember being greatly challenged by an Anglo-Catholic priest from the East End of London who came to our clergy gathering and spoke on evangelism. I thought I knew a bit about the subject, but that day I was deeply humbled by this man's dedication, and the question he set for us to discuss has ever since been seared on my heart: 'Do I burn with a passion, that is almost a pain, to bring people to Christ?'

Ways forward

So, if I do have that burning passion, how can I motivate my congregation for evangelism? Here are seven ways that I have found helpful.

1. **I must model this passion for evangelism.** It is no good expecting other members of the congregation to do what I myself am not prepared to do. But if I do model it, before long others will want to join in. I think of my debates with atheists, street preaching in Peckham, baptizing people in the river, leading mission teams, or sitting alongside enquirers and pointing them to Christ. In each case, my taking the initiative has encouraged others to want to be involved in something similar. When appointed to St Aldate's Church, I met the student group very early on. Before leaving, I mentioned that I would be doing some street preaching outside the church next day, a busy Saturday afternoon. The self-appointed leader of the group replied, 'We do not do street preaching at

St Aldate's.' I realized this was a critical moment, and said,
'Well, we are doing it tomorrow, and I expect you to be there.'
To his credit he was, and now he is a clergyman himself!

2. **I must teach this passion for evangelism.** Many clergy
exhort their congregations to be outward looking. And many
congregations think that this is what they pay their minister
for. And so nothing much gets done by either side. As a leader,
I need to teach the congregation, patiently and persistently,
that it is the job of all Christians to reach out to others. Some
may be able to speak in public about Christ. Some may, like
the wives mentioned in 1 Peter 3:1, be able by their very way
of life to win someone else to the Lord. But all should be able
to bear testimony to the Lord whom they love. All Christians
should be able to give substance to those three little mono-
syllables: 'I have found'. So the congregation needs to learn
that evangelism in some form or other is the responsibility of
the whole church, although some people will be particularly
gifted at it.

I recall my days at St Aldate's with much joy and gratitude.
To begin with, when I preached evangelistically, I invited
people who had made a response to come and see me personally at the end of the service. Later, I encouraged them to speak
to one of the staff or the person who had brought them. But
by the end of my time, I had such confidence in the ability
and zeal of the congregation to evangelize, that after making
an appeal I asked everyone to stand up and chat to those in
the nearby seats about where they stood with Christ. If folk
in their row had not taken a step of faith yet, I encouraged
Christians in the congregation to help them. I wandered
around the church myself, giving help when asked. It was such

a joy to see that members of the congregation had grown to the point where they could very naturally lead an enquirer to the Lord.

3. **I must persevere in this passion for evangelism.** Modelling it on one or two occasions is not good enough. The congregation must know that this outreach business is in my DNA, that 'woe to me if I do not preach the gospel'. Of course, there are countless ways of doing it. We will look at some of the more obvious ones below. But a few of the less obvious ways come to mind. I think of a carol service which I ended with an encouragement to decide for Christ. My closing words were: 'Not to decide, is to decide.' The words burnt into the heart of one man present, and some time later he told me that they had led him to Christ. On another occasion, we joined with a Pentecostal church to celebrate Easter in a holistic way. We had an evangelistic address, and then we broke for a meal that was already laid out on trestle tables at the side of the church. In the course of that break for mingling and eating, I led one person to Christ and a colleague led another. We then baptized several new believers, and ended with a profoundly moving Communion, accompanied by testimonies from various members, and much joy and praise of God, including (to the surprise of some!) singing in tongues.

4. **I must share this passion for evangelism.** I must never allow it to be thought that evangelism is the preserve of the minister or of the most gifted evangelist in the church. From my earliest days in the ministry, I learnt to take a little team with me on a youth outreach in another church. The newest Christian might get up and say that he or she had recently come to Christ, another might offer a prayer, and perhaps another

would take part of the talk. But all would return home, full of joy and having grown, because they had given out to others.

And of course two things happen, quite apart from any response to Christ. The receiving youth group begins to feel, 'Well, I rather liked that. I think we could do something similar ourselves.' And when news is given about the visit in the sending church's notices the following Sunday, other people in the congregation ask if they too can be taken on another occasion. And so the good infection spreads. I recall how, after a mission in Penticton, Canada, the youth were so fired up that they went up the valley on a mission trip of their own!

5. **I must vary the expression of this passion for evangelism.** There are countless ways of doing this. Adult baptisms, with the candidate giving a testimony to Christ, often stimulate interest among invited friends and relations, which can lead in due course to conversions. Then there can be celebration events such as a Valentine's dance or a hog roast, or an event based round sport or music, both very attractive to the general population. Needless to say, such occasions can include some presentation of the gospel appropriate to the setting. Drama is a powerful tool, and sometimes a short dramatic sketch is effective by itself in finalizing a decision for Christ. The parish holiday always draws in some who are perhaps married to Christians, but not there themselves yet. It can be a relaxed and happy way of considering the claims of Christ over the course of a week, and time and again I have found it effective. Practical acts of service and kindness can get through to people who have become cynical of words or of the lives of some professing Christians they know. And there are all sorts of possibilities in the home – discussions, Bible studies, parties, outreach suppers

and so forth. You never find Jesus approaching people in the Gospels in an identical way. He always employs variety. So we too must vary our approach imaginatively.

6. **I must train for evangelism.** There are many evangelism training courses. *Breaking News* and *Calling Out*, both by J.John, together with James Lawrence's *Lost for Words*, are among the courses most widely used in Britain. The trouble is that people are very willing to go on such courses, but very unwilling actually to get involved. I was leading an Evangelism Task Force for the emerging Anglican Church in the US, and I found precisely this trouble. So our team did a bit of teaching, and then got everyone out into the streets and shopping malls to put it into practice. The enthusiasm when people returned, in stark contrast to the panic in which they set out, was a joy to behold. Once, when teaching on evangelism in a theological college, I told the students, who had arrived somewhat bored with their notebooks, to put them all away because we would not be using them. We were to go out, two by two, into the surrounding streets and ask anyone we met what we could pray for, for them. This led to some magnificent encounters.

We need to train, but our training must include practical exposure in the real world. These encounters bring encouragement and the feeling that, for all my fears, 'I can do it'.

7. **I must nurture it.** Evangelism without subsequent nurture is sinful. It is like bringing a child to birth and leaving it to lie, untended, on the bed. The New Testament tells us that, when someone comes to faith, it is nothing less than a new birth, and babies need nourishment. What is more, they need food they can digest. So it is no good just inviting them to church and hoping they can cope. They probably will not

be able to. They will need to be lovingly looked after, and there must be adequate follow-up. And as the minister draws other members of the congregation into the exciting task of looking after new believers, the passion for evangelism and the belief that it is possible grow throughout the church.

How can the local church reach out?

Once motivated, what are some of the ways in which the church can reach beyond its borders?

Intentional prayer is one way. In many churches there is not much sign of intentional prayer for unconverted friends. But it is essential to bring specific names before God in intercession. The church in the majority world, where the gospel is growing so fast, depends on prayer. In the West we tend to rely on methods and technology. Often, we do not receive because we do not ask (James 4:2). We must not forget that it is God who is the evangelist. That is why prayer is so important. It expresses our utter dependence on him.

Testimony has always been important, because Christianity is more an experience of the living God than theory about him. But today testimony is more significant than ever before because of the prevalent postmodern culture and the widespread impression that Christianity is finished. All believers have a story of the interaction of their lives with Jesus Christ. Testimony asserts that Jesus is alive and can be met today. Many church members are afraid of being defeated in argument, and so they keep quiet. But they need not fear. The 'I-have-found' type of testimony is as unanswerable as it is unexpected. Nobody can rubbish your personal experience. Instead it may provoke in your friend the search for something similar.

I remember leading to Christ a young and almost illiterate man who worked in a slaughterhouse. It was during a mission, and in the evening service he got up and with stumbling simplicity told us he had found Jesus only that morning, and it was proving wonderful. His words had a great impact, and they stimulated others to bear witness.

Invitation. Many outreach events are spoiled because people do not invite their friends. Of course, if invitation is to be effective, there is a cost to pay. There must be an attractive lifestyle, time spent developing relationships, hospitality and shared interests. But given this preparation, you can invite individuals to a suitable event and as often as not expect a 'Yes'. Not because they particularly want to come to the event, but because they want to please you! Random invitations rarely work. We need to build bridges. 'Do go' does not work. 'Do come with me' often does.

I think of a top lawyer in North Carolina who is a great friend of mine. He was invited time after time to a business-men's Bible study, and steadfastly refused. But one day he gave in. It led to his conversion, and he has become an outstanding Christian. There are people out there who would come to a good Christian event – but nobody has ever invited them!

Courses such as Alpha, Christianity Explored or, more basic still, the Y Course, are currently among the most effective forms of outreach a church can lay on, provided people can be persuaded to taste them for themselves. Such courses suit postmodern culture, which is suspicious of authority figures, disenchanted with institutions, doubtful about truth claims, confused about personal identity, looking for reality, short on hope, yet hungry for spiritual experience.

Alpha's strapline, 'Exploring the meaning of life', grabs people. So does the food, the humour, the quality videos, the companionship, the freedom to question and the weekend away. To be effective, any of these courses needs to be complemented with good pastoral care.

Hospitality. Jesus knew he was touching one of the deepest strains in human nature when he left us a meal to remember him with. A good meal breaks down suspicion, encourages openness, and makes people receptive. Events based around food tend to work remarkably well. You need a speaker who has charm, directness and tact. You need an engaging subject. You need a nice meal. Naturally you will want to have a nurture group in place, to steer people into after the event, if appropriate. I find this method of evangelism over food one of the most fruitful of all approaches today, and I use it a lot.

I remember my wife and I invited a couple to our home. We were discussing the most exciting discovery we had ever made. I was dishing out ice-cream and chocolate sauce for the dessert when it came to my turn. I said, 'My greatest discovery is that Jesus Christ is alive and you can know him – have some more chocolate sauce?' The ensuing conversation in due course led to their conversion!

Guest services. The guest service was, I think, the invention of John Stott. It was certainly one of the earliest of modern attempts at evangelism. Its plan was simple: to invite people on the fringe of the congregation to a service shorn of unhelpful elements, and thereby bring them a gospel message appropriate to their situation. It required a lot of careful preparation, an evocative title, good publicity, an enthusiastic and inviting congregation, much prayer, the use of testimony, familiar music, and a challenging talk designed to bring waverers to a decision. It is still effective, though because most people are further away from Christianity than they used to be and need more time to decide, the challenge is frequently to join an enquiry group rather than come to Christ there and then. A good guest service, put on perhaps three times a year, can be a very effective tool.

Leisure-based events, such as a golf tournament or football match, a sports day, a skiing holiday, hill walking, or sailing, draw people together, particularly if there is some risk or danger involved. And in this context, people can be attracted to Christ. Any shared event will do. I have even found dominoes and a gardening group to be effective in direct evangelism!

Evangelism in the home. This could include an invitation to supper and conversation on an interesting topic. It could be a group invitation, to hear and interact with a speaker, engage in an investigative Bible study or share in an enquirers' group. An interesting person could be invited to speak on 'My God and my job'. The very location in the home makes things much easier and more intimate. Jesus used the home a lot, and so could we.

Visiting is a proven method of discovering needs, engaging interest, and sometimes of taking the person to the point of conversion, but it almost seems to have died out. However, it can still open doors for evangelism. Young people have shown the way. YWAM[1] and OM[2] both major on visiting and the use of questionnaires in the streets, or offering Christian literature in shops and malls. In the US, Evangelism Explosion is based on visiting. In the UK, Dan Cozens has for many years led a Walk of 1000 Men, based on pubs throughout a specified area. It is not strictly parochial, but many men from parishes throughout the country join his teams for visiting, small meetings, conversations in pubs, art displays and so forth. The participants are fed by local Christians, have only £5 in their pockets (to buy someone a drink), and sleep on church floors. Needless to say, they are inspired by Jesus' mission of the seventy, and are the modern embodiment of it.

Community service is one of the best ways in which a local church can make an impact on its area. The church needs to analyse where the need is, and then seek to supply it, whether through prison visiting, adoption services, soup kitchens, indoor football, a church coffee shop or restaurant, support for the aged, or whatever. Not only is this Christlike service, but it also wins us the right to be heard. People inevitably wonder why we offer something for free like this. If they ask us, this gives us a marvellous opportunity to explain something of the gospel. Freely we have received, freely we give.

The mission week or weekend is an excellent way, both to serve other localities and to bind our own team together in unforgettable fellowship. Complementary gifts among team members, testimonies, fellowship, the variety of personalities, all tend to carry conviction, and stimulate the receiving end to do likewise. It may be a large mission team. It may be just a car-full for a single event. It is invariably better than a solo outing. I believe the parish mission is forgotten dynamite, something I have commended and described in my book of the same name.[3] It can be highly effective for a church to invite a team led by a competent evangelist. Members spend a week in the homes of a church or collection of churches which have made proper preparations and have produced a wide variety of events. The receiving church is thrilled, and the visitors find that they grow spiritually through the experience.

There are countless other ways in which the church can spread the good news. One church I know ran a programme based on *Strictly Come Dancing*, another a regular discussion group for mothers who had dropped their kids off at school. Another ran *Any Questions* at a neutral venue; another offered prayer for healing in the street. Passion plays have been invaluable for centuries, and open-air drama-and-testimony events in busy places, accompanied by plenty of personal workers to chat with onlookers, can prove very effective. On the Move has proved itself as an international means of open-air outreach, with free barbecues, music, short talks and the chance to chat about the faith. We have one such event in Oxford every year, which draws – and feeds – some 5,000 individuals over the course of three extended lunchtimes. People are amazed to find that there is such a thing as a free lunch after all! Some of them discover more than this. But all of them agree that this is the sort of thing the church should be doing.

Imagination, prayer, passion, determination and every-member ministry – these are some of the qualities needed in the church that is alive to the needs of those beyond its doors. And in today's post-Christian society the more that can take place off church property, the less embarrassed people will be to attend.

Chapter 6

UNIVERSITY OUTREACH

Of all forms of Christian ministry, I love work among university students the best. They are so sharp, so engaged, so vibrant, and they have their lives before them. I was heavily involved in this work as a student myself, when President of the Christian Union at Oxford. I have been speaking to undergraduate audiences for fifty years now. I have led university missions in Oxford, Cambridge, Durham, London, Edinburgh, Sheffield, Newcastle, and elsewhere in the UK, and many in various countries overseas. I love being in the company of students, and although I am far too ancient, they still seem to invite me!

Students

The Christian students themselves are the key to outreach in the university. Benevolent academics and chaplains can be a great help, and both church and parachurch have their place. But the best work is always done by the students themselves.

They live cheek by jowl among the friends they hope to win for Christ. Their lives are either an attraction to, or a deterrent from, the Christian cause. Their behaviour is under more scrutiny than they recognize. I think there are probably some five areas where their influence is most felt.

Way of life

First is through the way they live. Of course, Christian students come up to the university at very different stages of development. Some arrive as robust, established Christians, glad to escape from the restrictions of school and be free to talk with all and sundry about their faith. Others have a less developed spirituality, and they are going to need all the help they can get from the Christian community in the university if they are to survive and grow. The two most obvious dangers for freshers are: to be inappropriately pushy about their Christianity, or to be so browbeaten by the secularist culture that they make fatal compromises early on and ruin any chance of making an impact. As lectures get underway, particularly in the scientific, theological or philosophical disciplines, sceptical professors can easily cow callow students and ridicule their faith. Such are the dangers, but once recognized, they can readily be circumvented. Moreover, the quality of life displayed by the Christian students – their helpfulness, their sense of fun, their integrity, their language – must adorn the gospel they profess to follow.

Involvement

Secondly, it is important for Christian students to throw themselves into the life of the university. They need to be seen in the various university clubs and sports, in the junior common rooms and in the bar – yes, even if they elect to go for soft drinks. Salt is no good if it is kept in the salt cellar. And Christians are called to be salt to their society and come 'out of the saltshaker', to cite the title of Becky Pippert's splendid book.[1] It is sad when you see Christians all eating at the same table in hall, and creeping away to the weekly Bible study while failing to engage meaningfully with the non-Christians around them. No wonder they can earn the reputation for being wet.

Lack of embarrassment

There is a third area. If the student is fun to be with, and unembarrassed about Christianity ('Yes indeed, I am a Christian. Aren't you?'), others will be curious. Many eighteen-year-olds imagine that Christianity is for old fogies, and that none of their bright, intelligent peers would ever get involved in something so uncool. It will amaze them to find attractive, natural Christians in their midst, and when they do, they are sure to ask about it. That is the opportunity for the Christians to say just a word or two about what Jesus means to them. They need to major on Jesus, and on the fact that he is alive and relevant. Probably their colleagues had imagined that Christianity is about drab church buildings with musty smells, or dreary moral regulations. They may not realize that it is essentially about this exciting person, Jesus, and the difference he can make to anyone's life. It is important for the Christian student not to say too much at this stage – just bear witness to a living Jesus. If the other person wants to know more, he or she will ask. If not, there is no point in pushing more down his or her throat! Wait for a better opportunity.

Invitations

A fourth way in which Christian students can serve Christ effectively is to give appropriate invitations. This will demand the prior building of bridges of friendship (as we saw in the last chapter), but given that, a well-judged invitation can lead, and has led, to the conversion of many a student. You must choose your event and speaker with care, judging what is likely to be most helpful. If your friendship with the person in question is strong enough, he (or she) will make the effort to come in order to please you. If not, he (or she) will produce a variety of reasons why he cannot make it! Students will not come just by reading notices. They probably will not come if someone older from church invites them. But they may well come if one of their peers does so with enthusiasm and charm.

Personal conversations

The other way in which students can make an impact is by praying for a close friend who is not a Christian, and then taking the opportunity for a personal talk with him or her about Jesus Christ. I led a number of student friends to Christ when I was an undergraduate. People are more open to new ideas when they are students than they are likely to be in later life. For the Christian student who knows the heart of the good news and can communicate it with simplicity and warmth, this is one of the best ways of Christian service while still at university.

But although the students themselves are key operators in university outreach, they are not the only ones.

The role of the local church

The local church has a part to play too. Not every church is suited to student outreach, but a number, situated in university cities, make this an important part of their programme, deliberately setting out to be agents in the conversion and nurture of students in the adjoining university.

Students live busy lives with weekday commitments, so the main way in which they can be reached by a local church is through Sunday services. Lively worship, generous hospitality and good teaching are the key ingredients. A sense of the reality of God's presence is vital in the worship. I do not think it needs to be wildly avant-garde. Indeed, there is even a tendency among quite a lot of students these days to hanker for a more liturgical style of worship!

But whatever the style, it has to be authentic. Our Oxford church used the methods cited in the previous chapter. We ran a late-evening event each Sunday, with one of us debating with a celebrated figure from the trades unions, government or academia. And the mix seemed to be effective and draw hundreds of students to the church. We would follow morning worship with a student lunch and short topical presentation, and that had considerable appeal. Students live institutional lives and are often glad for the hospitality of a home. Some will join home fellowship groups or teach in the Sunday schools, though their main focus at this stage in their lives should be in their college.

The use of testimony in church or other outreach meetings needs some thought. Traditionally someone stands up before the main speaker gets going, and tells how unsatisfying their life was before they came to Christ, how the change took place, and what the sequel has been. That is not a bad plan, but it sounds unreal and pretentious if someone gets up unprompted to say these very personal things. It is much better if the service leader or preacher interviews the person. The person being interviewed is therefore more relaxed, does not have to learn any little speech, and the whole thing comes over more naturally.

I tend to do an interview in the course of my talk, not as a prelude. It is unexpected, it offers a change of voice, and it underlines the point I am making about the transforming power of Christ. Needless to say, the impact among students when one of their peers is interviewed in this way is considerable!

My predecessor at St Aldate's devised a brilliant plan for the year, which I was glad to follow. The first term was largely devoted to evangelism, the second to teaching, and the third to preparing students to go on a big mission, as part of a team of about 100 or 150, in the September. This, of course, took a lot of planning, particularly among the receiving churches in the town we went to, and required the serious training of our own students. But it was invaluable. Students of all levels of spirituality could come. Often we had young men and women who had been Christians for only a few weeks. But they grew tremendously as they saw the gospel winning people, not just in university situations, but in ordinary secular life. And they returned for the next autumn term, full of enthusiasm to reach out to the new batch of undergraduates.

There are several ways in which a local church can complement the outreach that the students themselves carry out in college. First, the church can offer a clear plan of evangelistic preaching which the students are familiar with. This means they can confidently invite their friends to come with them. On the first four Sundays of the autumn term, we were unashamedly evangelistic, and often those weeks produced more than a hundred new believers, whom we nourished for the remainder of the term in nurture groups (which I will discuss more fully in the final chapter). Secondly, the church was able to train the students for evangelism. We had regular training courses for this purpose, based round food! Then, thirdly, we would do evangelism with them. This took place not just in missions away from Oxford, but in the colleges themselves. My colleagues and I were frequently invited into colleges by Christian students to give a talk in the bar and host a discussion on some topical aspect of the faith, and often one or two students would come to Christ through such evenings. These events formed a regular part of the partnership in evangelism between the church and the students. They would not have had the speakers without us, and we would not have had the audience without them.

The presence of Muslim students in British universities is increasing all the time. Many Christian students tend to avoid them, feeling they are too difficult a proposition to engage in spiritual conversation! But others take the better route, that of friendship. In Oxford and Cardiff, for example, a loose-knit organization called *Mahabba* ('Welcome' in Arabic) has emerged, and is spreading to other university cities too. Concerned individuals from a dozen churches come together to pray, and to befriend students walking around pedestrian precincts who clearly come from the Middle East. They invite them to homes, to meals, to football games, to videos, in short to see what Christian church or exploratory Bible studies can be like. They make Bibles available in their own languages, if required, and invite their Muslim contacts to appropriate church events. Many from countries such as Saudi Arabia, Libya and Yemen have never seen a Bible, met a Christian, or entered a church building. It was like that with Chinese students too a while ago. This friendly approach is obviously the right way to proceed, time-consuming though it is. Some Christians in a church or university feel a special calling to it, and some have the requisite linguistic ability, which is an enormously attractive asset. This warm, interpersonal approach leads to the dispelling of suspicion, clear appreciation of what the different faiths hold in common and where they diverge, and the opportunity to learn and reflect. Many of these Muslim students will return to their countries to occupy leadership positions, with a much warmer appreciation of Christianity. What is more, every year some of them come to faith and baptism, immensely costly though this is in terms of their own family relationships.

Having spent a good many years leading a church in a university city with large numbers of students attending, I have reflected a good deal on the relationship between the church and the university Christian Union. It seems to me undeniable that the best people to get alongside students are indeed other students. As a church leader in a student setting, therefore, I always encouraged students to get involved in the Christian Union, because it gives them unique opportunities for mission. The CU as a student-led society has a reach into the campus that is just not available to a church, especially in these days of secularist attacks on our freedom to proclaim the gospel. I have also observed that students who worked together in mission, acknowledging differences in their theology, but standing together in unity on the essentials, learnt a great deal from one another. This approach to mission and unity has been of real benefit to the church in the UK.

The prime role, therefore, of the local church should be to support and build up the Christians in their colleges. But it can also offer high-quality apologetics events or evangelistic talks to which the students can bring their friends. It can run vacation activities, such as reading weeks or missions in its own country or overseas. It can offer the sacraments of baptism and Holy Communion which students themselves are not authorized to do. The main principle is for the church to have the humility to offer what the Christian groups in the university cannot, and to supplement their outreach as needed. For example, we used to run a very informal midweek early morning Communion and address, followed by breakfast, before lectures. Scores of students found this a great blessing, and naturally it could not have been done by their Christian Union. We baptized new believers among the students, some of whom wanted immersion, which we were glad to offer in the local river – causing intense interest and curiosity among the people on the bank and the boats on the river! And leaders of the Christian groups will come to the church leaders for advice, if relations are good. In a word, the work of the Christian groups and the churches need not interfere or clash with each other, but should rather complement each other.

The university's chaplain and parachurch agencies

In England, chaplains are appointed by practically all universities, and in some residential universities by the individual colleges as well. These are normally Church of England clergy, male or female, often supplemented by part-time chaplains from other denominations or religions. Their role is to offer general care to all students, an open ear to listen to their needs, and the willingness to help in any way they can. They also run the official chapel meetings for the college or university. This puts them in a difficult position. The students, with all the arrogance of eighteen-year-olds, tend to write them off. They are part of the establishment, and so are mildly suspect. They are rarely evangelical in outlook, and accordingly are even more suspect! On the other hand, the academics often tend to look down on chaplains as social workers committed to a God who does not exist. So chaplains can often have a lonely existence, running very small services, primarily attended by a choir. They tend to despise the Christian Union as fundamentalist, and the Christian Union returns the compliment! But surely the Christian students should give encouragement to the chaplain, and show their Christian commitment by attending chapel from time to time? And the chaplain should befriend the Christian Union, and maybe sit at the back of some of their meetings to show support for their Christianity, even if they do not share their theology? It is not easy to be a university chaplain.

Another support for Christian students in British universities is the supply of staff workers from the UCCF, a strongly evangelical and evangelistic organization spanning the denominations, whose work is becoming increasingly influential. When I was an undergraduate, the Student Christian Movement, with a more liberal interpretation of Christianity and a more social orientation, was very influential in universities, but now it has vanished without trace. UCCF is now the main parachurch organization in universities, with others such as Agape (ex-Campus Crusade) seeking to gain a following. UCCF pioneered the Christian Unions in the universities as non-denominational mission teams, led by students. Christian Unions are affiliated to UCCF, and are supported by staff workers who are usually graduates and therefore themselves recent members of Christian Unions. This gives them an easy rapport with students. They speak at many small meetings, lunch bars and coffee parties by invitation. They give advice to Christian Union leaders. They spend a great deal of time caring pastorally for individuals. They invite the student Christian leadership to big inter-university training courses in the vacations. They have no official role within the structure of the university, being financed and appointed from outside, but they provide a valuable voluntary support for the Christian Unions, and their advice is often sought on issues which Christian students feel passionately about, such as suitable speakers, spiritual gifts, cooperation with other Christian bodies, the place of women in leadership, or how 'sound' such and such a church might be. The danger is that they can influence the student executive committee too much, and often in the single direction of their own theological convictions! And whereas academics can laugh off the activities of zealous undergraduates in the Christian Union, they are often much more suspicious of organized influences from outside, like UCCF staff workers, who therefore need to do their work very discreetly. The climate is getting more chilly: in some universities, Christians are no longer allowed to meet on campus, whereas rooms are made available in which the Muslim or Buddhist students may gather.

The university mission

A few decades ago, the Christian Unions in most universities would organize a major mission on a triennial basis. Nowadays it tends to be an annual affair, in February or March. This is seen as the main plank in the evangelism. In universities where there is a large Christian Union, the mission may last a week, embracing both Sundays. Elsewhere, it usually lasts from Monday to Friday. The whole thing is carefully planned. A major consideration is the choice of the main missioner. He or she needs to be a good evangelist and an able apologist, because there will certainly be plenty of assaults on the Christian position. There will also be a team of associates, many of them UCCF workers from other parts of the country, younger clergy or lay assistants who have a gift for evangelism. Their job is normally to encourage the Christian group, and address small meetings for their not-yet-Christian friends.

The main activities will be a daily lunch event, with free food and literature, a powerful talk by the missioner, questions, and lots of one-to-one conversations afterwards. In the evening it is much the same, though the programme will be more imaginative and there may be no food! Sometimes the evening event is more directly evangelistic, while at lunchtime the more common objections to the Christian faith are addressed. The key to a successful week remains what it always was: prayer and mobilizing the Christian students to invite their friends. Without these guests, visitors are powerless. But if students bring their friends, the sky is the limit to what can be achieved.

I particularly recall a mission I led in Oxford University. The Christian Union had acquired the Sheldonian Theatre, the largest building in the university, for the evening meetings.

Jazz was playing as people entered, and each night there was a fascinating testimony from someone well known to the student body. When preparing my talks, I had three different types of people in mind. I knew that some would be apathetic and need to be startled into interest. Others would be sceptical and need to be convinced. A third lot would be hedonistic and need to be challenged. The talk each night had to address all three!

There was always a challenge to commitment at the end of each talk. You might feel that this is overkill, but I think that the problem can be overcome. I tend to say, 'Some of you may entirely reject what I have said. You may think Christianity is a load of rubbish. OK, I challenge you to look at the evidence for the Christian claim', and point them to a free Gospel and perhaps an apologetic book. I continue, 'Some of you are interested, but not persuaded. Right, let me encourage you to pursue the quest. Sign up for one of the enquiry courses that will start when this week is over.' And I impress on the assistant missioners the necessity of taking the names and encouraging people who are listening to sign up. Finally, I say, 'For some of you, today may have been particularly significant. You may have decided to start following Christ. Please be sure to meet one of the team and jot down your name on the response card on your seat, because you are going to need help in the days ahead.'

On every seat there would be an attractively produced response card, inviting students to a series of follow-up talks. As they would leave, people would hand in these cards at the door, and gradually the number would mount. Some 230 had committed themselves to these follow-up sessions by the end of that Oxford mission week, but this rapidly grew to about 400, as not-yet-Christians sang the praises of the follow-up course to their friends, who then began to accompany them! Part of the secret of this impact was a prayer meeting that met in the basement of the Sheldonian each night, praying for the proclamation of the gospel that was going on above their heads.

It is impossible to overemphasize the place of prayer in evangelism. I once led a mission in Cambridge University, when I was Principal of St John's Theological College, Nottingham. To my amazement, more than a thousand attended each night, but the response was very small. On the penultimate night, a staff colleague at my theological college had a dream. It was a World War 1 setting, and I was going over the top, while my mates, who had promised covering fire, were just playing cards in the trenches and offering no support. The meaning was pretty obvious, so this staff member organized a chain of prayer throughout the day. That night, the last of the mission, more than a hundred undergraduates professed commitment to Christ, and we had a great follow-up breakfast the next morning. I have never forgotten it. It impressed on me the centrality of prayer in evangelism.

Sometimes missions lead to unplanned encounters. I think of a sharp debate that I took part in with communist students in Auckland University, or with students passionate for freedom in Durham. I think of an amazing proclamation of the gospel in Cape Town University, on the back of a massive anti-apartheid gathering, and in the University of North Carolina, following a packed debate with an atheist professor. Another took place in Southampton University during a student sit-in protesting against the administration department. I think of three days of outreach at Oxford University by Billy Graham, at my invitation, when Billy was heckled, and members of the University Anarchist Society got on to the roof of the Town Hall where he was speaking and cut the land-lines to five other locations to which the event was being televised! Such occasions seem to produce the most fruit for the cause of Christ.

Here is an account of one of the most imaginative missions held in a British university in 2010. It began with a remarkable outpouring of the Holy Spirit at a house party in the vacation before the mission, where students really 'fell in love with Jesus'. This was crucial, and led to fervent prayer among them before the mission, continuing into 24-7 prayer throughout the mission itself. The chief student leader gathered around himself people with a big vision for the university, clever networkers and students with wide circles of non-Christian friends. The outcome was highly creative.

For one thing, they opted for a lot of decentralized events which really made the week come alive. There was no single 'big-name' evangelist, but the diverse gifts of the assistants ('CU guests', as they were called) were used to the full. They went into the houses of the students and spoke at dinner parties, tea parties, events where Christians were grilled by all comers, film evenings, pudding parties and so forth. At these parties the host explained that there would be a five-minute talk after the meal, followed by discussion and coffee – often far into the night. The main missioner acted more as an encourager and father figure to the team than as the single oracle, in striking contrast to the way these things are usually done. A student friend of mine, who was an assistant on this mission, tells me that she had the chance to speak to more than 200 students about the good news of Jesus during the week, because of the initiative students took in inviting friends to small events, and also because of the trust and freedom given them by the main missioner.

Naturally, they had the normal lunch and major evening events as well. But daily they ran a lot of street questionnaires, helped by the desire of a local newspaper to publish a survey of 1,000 students about God. So the assistant missioners had plenty to do during the day, and, by taking students with them, they developed the timid and boosted the confidence of younger Christians. They organized 'whitewash teams' which went to clean grubby student kitchens and bathrooms, serving the community by showing the love of Christ in a practical way. The visiting team lived among the students, which was very important for establishing and developing relationships, many of which bore fruit in conversions as the week progressed. Needless to say, after a mission of this quality they had many takers for the follow-up course which began the next week.

There is no one ideal way of running missions, no one preordained style. At one I led recently, the students had not been able to acquire a suitable room, so we set up shop with couches, screens and food in the main corridor of the university, where an endless stream of people passed by. It was an eerie experience, starting to preach when there was practically nobody there, but within a few minutes the whole corridor was blocked by a crowd of people gathering to listen. The vital elements are prayer, a winsome and fearless presentation of the faith, massive student enthusiasm and involvement and, as always in student work, food! Much depends on careful preparation beforehand, and on the equally careful follow-up of the two classes of people who leave their names: those who have decided for Christ, and those who are interested but not persuaded. But in today's climate, the annual mission remains a powerful tool for university outreach.

Chapter 7

CARELESS TALK

We have looked at the main content of the good news, and how it can be proclaimed in church and university situations, which are the main areas in which I have worked. Now I want to pause and look with some care at the language in which this good news is commonly expressed. Often we still find Christians, and particularly preachers, using what is sometimes called 'the language of Zion', understood in Christian circles, but misleading or meaningless beyond them.

'You are born in sin,' they say – but what might that mean? 'Come to the cross,' they say – but how do you do that? Your destiny is to be 'washed in the blood of the Lamb' – it sounds disgusting. Using technical language to communicate with the general public is a great mistake, and it is not just Christians who are guilty of it. Doctors and scientists often make the same mistake. So if we have any desire to spread the good news of Jesus, we need to use simple, evocative language which will really get our message through to people who have no background in the Bible, church, or even in Christianity generally.

Back in the days of World War 2, there was a series of short injunctions from the government, such as 'dig for victory' or 'careless talk costs lives'. Certainly in wartime, careless talk can easily cost lives. And I think careless Christian talk can do much the same. We can give a totally false impression by some of the words we use. In this chapter I'm going to take a look at three: 'converted', 'born again' and 'saved', the stock in trade of the evangelist, and often misused and misunderstood.

'I've been converted!'

We have all heard it. Sometimes it is an arrogant, but often a joyful, cry. It is readily understood when applied to someone who moves from one religion to another, or from no faith to a definite belief. But what can it mean when it is applied, as it so often is, to people who have been brought up in a vaguely Christian context and have now committed themselves to Christ and his way of life?

It may help us to turn to the Greek word used in the New Testament: *epistrephein*. It means 'to turn'. Actually the noun 'conversion' only occurs once, can you believe it? It is used in Acts 15:3 of the 'conversion' of the Gentiles. But the way the verb is used is highly instructive. It is never used in the passive, as we use it, to 'be converted'. It is always active. Sometimes it is used in a transitive sense (we can 'turn' people to God: Luke 1:16; James 5:19), often intransitively (thus we are said to 'turn' to him ourselves as in Luke 22:32; Acts 11:21 and so on). God himself is frequently used as the subject of this verb. He 'turns' people to himself.

Let's take it a bit further. In the New Testament both repentance and faith are called 'turning'. In repentance you turn from wickedness (Acts 3:26), from pagan ways (Acts 15:19), from darkness to light, and from the power of Satan to God (Acts 26:18). And there is a sombre thought: you can turn back again, like a dog to its vomit or a pig to its wallowing in the mud (2 Peter 2:22). Faith, on the other hand, is seen as 'turning' to the Lord (Mark 4:12; Acts 3:19 and so on). It is, if you like, returning to the Shepherd of our souls (1 Peter 2:25).

That is how the word we use for 'being converted' is used in the New Testament. You can turn someone else to God, or turn to him yourself. And that turning involves repentance and faith. That, coupled with baptism (the physical sign of belonging), is the human side of becoming a Christian. There is a divine side, called by a variety of names, among them 'new birth', which we will look at in a moment.

But let's stay with conversion for the moment. How should we preach for it? A careful study of the sermons in Acts shows that the first Christians seem to have used a fourfold pattern, doubtless with many variations. First, they discerned the need among the people they were speaking to. It might be danger, fear, loneliness, sin, or something like spiritual blindness. Secondly, they proclaimed a person, Jesus Christ himself, who shares God's nature as well as ours, and died on the cross to rescue us from sin. Thirdly, they offered a gift: forgiveness and the Holy Spirit. And finally they looked for a response. Nothing less than turning from the old ways to such a marvellous Saviour would do. Such was conversion, the gateway into the Christian community.

On any showing, conversion is a very extensive term. There is conversion to Christ, when you become a child of God. That is the personal side of conversion. There is conversion to the church, when you join the people of God, the corporate side of conversion. And there is, in a proper sense, conversion to the world, when you start extending the reign of God in other lives, the public aspect of conversion.

We are now in a position to answer some questions about conversion.

Here's the first question: *Is conversion sudden or gradual?* Not a very good question, though it is often asked! As we saw in the case of Peter and Paul in chapter 2, it can be gradual but it can also be sudden. God uses both crisis and process in his work of drawing us to himself. The real question is not so much, 'When did you join?' as 'Do you belong?'; not so much 'When were you born?' as 'Are you alive?'

Here's a second question: *Is conversion God's work or ours?* As we have seen, it is we who turn. But the turning is God's work too, and that is stressed no less than fifteen times in the New Testament! So perhaps the King James Version's mistranslation 'Be converted', although poor linguistics, is good theology after all!

But *is conversion a matter of experience or action?* Remember, the verb is active, never passive. It is not so much an experience you feel, as an action you take. You turn. And the New Testament sees this turning not in psychological, but in dynamic terms. It involves an act of will and surrender.

Finally, *how lasting is conversion?* Conversion means turning and committing yourself to that lifelong union with Christ which baptism symbolizes: union with him in death, which brings freedom from the prison of sin, and in resurrection, which brings his power into our lives. It means reckoning that union with Christ is a fact – and acting accordingly.

'Have you been born again?'

That is a somewhat threatening question which is often asked. I think we can deal with this one more easily. If you live in America, it can very easily be misunderstood. There are millions of so-called 'born again' people who stand on the political right, but their Christianity is often more political than religious. The word can be misunderstood in the UK as well. There is a strand in some church teaching which maintains that, if you have been baptized, even as a tiny infant, and even if you totally reject the Christian faith, then you are necessarily born again. There is no such automatic action with God. You can't be 'born again' unless you want to be.

The word 'born again' is identical with 'regenerate' in the Greek. It speaks of a radical new beginning. It is one of a group of words like justification, baptism, conversion, adoption, receiving the Spirit, which all in their different ways speak of our initial entry into God's family. Regeneration, or the new birth, is not a particularly common way of describing it in the New Testament, but it does occur in a number of places, in the writings of John, Paul, Peter and James. It means God breathing new life into us, or putting his Spirit into us when we 'turn' to him in repentance and faith. Christian initiation is like a rope with three strands. The personal strand is repentance and faith. The churchly strand is baptism. The divine strand is the new birth. They all belong together. I am a Christian when I have come to the Lord in repentance and faith, have received his gift of the life-giving Holy Spirit into my very being, and have publicly acknowledged it in the sacrament Jesus gave us: baptism. So the question 'Have you been born again?' really means 'Have you come to Christ in repentance and faith, as baptism symbolizes, and received his life-giving Spirit?' It is quite an apt question among people who have been in church circles for a long time but show no signs of being set alight by Christ. But it is not necessarily the most tactful question with which to approach them! Nor is the claim to be born again proof of true Christian discipleship. True birth leads on to appropriate living!

'I was saved last Sunday!'

I love it when I hear that, because I know what the person means. But if we are to be faithful to the New Testament, it will never do, and preachers should not encourage it. Not only does it seem very strange and even threatening language to those who are not part of the evangelical subculture, but it is at odds with the teaching of the Bible. The word 'save' has a wealth of meanings in Scripture, including to rescue, to win victory, to bring new life, to offer fulfilment. I wrote a book about it some years ago, *The Meaning of Salvation*,[1] and at the end of that book I was convinced of the simple truth that I was taught in my early twenties: salvation has three tenses, a past, a present and a future.

The *past* tense of salvation tells me that I have been saved or rescued from the penalty of sin by Christ's death on the cross, and my response to it.

It is something I can be confident of. Christ's awesome action there was sufficient and complete, and it never needs to be repeated. Occasionally, very occasionally in the New Testament, that past tense is used. Ephesians 2:8 is perhaps the most famous: 'For it is by grace you have been saved, through faith.' Romans 8:24 uses that past tense again, but it has a future thrust to it. 'In this hope we were saved,' it says, and the hope is defined as the final redemption of our bodies. 2 Timothy 1:9f. uses the past tense (he 'saved us'), but it points to the future as well: the destruction of death and the bringing of immortality to light. It is much the same in the other reference: Titus 3:5–7. There again we read 'he saved us', but once again we have that forward look: 'so that . . . we might become heirs having the hope of eternal life'. So it is true to say, as we look back to the cross and resurrection, 'I have been saved.' But it is far from the whole story.

For the 'saved' word is much more commonly used in the *present* tense. A famous example is 1 Corinthians 1:18, where Paul maintains with joy that the message of the cross is 'to us who are being saved . . . the power of God', or 1 Corinthians 15:2, where the Greek reads: 'by this gospel you are being saved' (though the NIV obscures this!). This use of 'saved' in the present is common in the New Testament. We have been rescued by what Christ achieved once for all on the cross, and we continue to experience that salvation through the work of the Holy Spirit within us. He is the first instalment of our future inheritance (Ephesians 1:14). When we trust the power of the Holy Spirit, for example in temptation, we experience salvation, that is to say, rescue from sin and failure. When we don't trust him for it, we don't experience it.

However, the main way in which the 'saved' word is used in the New Testament refers to *the future* when God's great work for us is complete. The verses are plentiful. 'Through him we shall be saved'; 'We have been saved in hope . . . of the resurrection of the body'; 'Our salvation is nearer now than when we first believed'; and 'We wait for the blessed hope – the

glorious appearing of our great God and Saviour, Jesus Christ.'
In words like these, the future hope at the heart of salvation
echoes through the pages of the New Testament. That strong
hope, of course, is no wishful thinking, but is based fairly and
squarely on the resurrection, when Christ won that crucial
cosmic battle against sin and Satan. The decisive move in the
game of chess has been played, whether or not the opponent
realized its significance. The outcome is assured, although the
game has yet to be finished. It is the conclusion of the game
to which salvation looks. Salvation, like justification, belongs
properly to the Last Day, so we need therefore to be careful in
claiming, 'I have been saved' *tout simple*.

I find the analogy of a drowning man very helpful. The
watchful coastguard sees him struggling and sinking, and
at once sets out to rescue him in his speedboat. He pulls
him from the waves, and it is therefore quite true to say that
he has been saved. But he is not back yet. He is being saved
or kept afloat by the boat in which he is now lying, and it
would always be possible for him to jump out and drown,
but that would be the ultimate folly. Before long he will be
back ashore, when his salvation or rescue will be complete.
So there are three tenses in salvation. I can say, 'I have been
saved from the penalty of sin through Christ's death on the
cross. I am being saved from the power of sin by the indwelling Holy Spirit – when I trust him. And one day I will be
saved from the very presence of sin, when I die and see my
Lord face to face.' In the meantime, I must not anticipate the
future by assimilating it with the past tense of salvation and
giving the impression that I have it all now. The best is yet
to come.

I have given three examples of the way in which it is all too easy for evangelists to use language carelessly and unbiblically, and run the risk of causing considerable misunderstanding. We have all probably met some hedonist who says, 'Oh yes, I was saved when I was fourteen, so I am all right. I can go now and do what I like.' Scripture tells us very firmly that this is a false hope. There must always be an 'already' and a 'not yet' when we talk about salvation. Perhaps we need to work harder at finding language which expresses both what has already been achieved and also what lies ahead to be claimed. The New Testament writers use several expressions. A couple are 'adoption' and 'redemption'.

Adoption and redemption
Adoption means that a contract has been signed and is sure and unbreakable. I can know I am adopted into a family. But that is not all there is to it. I must gradually have my uncouth ways from my former life changed, and learn the standards and lifestyle of my new family. There is, therefore, a forward orientation to adoption. Interestingly, the apostle Paul warns us that our Christian adoption will be complete only at the Last Day (Romans 8:23). Adopted already, 'we ourselves, who have the firstfruits of the Spirit, groan inwardly as we wait eagerly for our adoption as sons, the redemption of our bodies'. In this profound verse, the apostle brings together not only the present and the future of our Christian lives, but the two ideas of adoption and redemption.

Redemption was often used as a commercial metaphor in the ancient world. You put a down payment on some piece of property to secure it as your own. You would return later to 'redeem' it fully. Perhaps if we used images like this more frequently, we would help people to see that their entry into the Christian life is not the end, but the beginning of what will be sustained by God's grace throughout life, and will culminate in heaven.

Yes, words matter, and we need to use them with care!

Chapter 8

ALL CHANGE!

When I went to Regent College, Vancouver, back in 1988 to
teach evangelism, I was soon invited on to a radio programme
with Shirley MacLaine to discuss her New Age ideas. I am
ashamed to say I declined, because I then knew next to
nothing about the revolution in thought and culture which
we now call postmodernism, and which has inevitably
changed our approach to evangelism. I was way behind the
times!

Modernism

It has never been easy to proclaim the gospel. When I began,
many years ago, I realized that there were major issues in the
culture to contend with. Perhaps the biggest overall problem
was the contemporary climate, where Christianity was a
dwindling force, a minority interest. It was – and remains – no
longer the backcloth to human life and thought, as it was in
the Middle Ages. The climate of the West has been profoundly
secularized. A number of factors account for this.

One was the rise of the European Renaissance during the fourteenth and fifteenth centuries. A whole new world of learning was released, springing from the culture of classical Greece and Rome: its art, philosophy, science, and above all, its humanism. Human beings, not God, became the measure of all things. This world, not the next, became the centre of attention. The Reformation in the sixteenth century brought an accompanying revolution in church and society, while the rise of the natural sciences, pioneered by men such as Copernicus and Galileo, liberated people from church dogma and opened up a spirit of empirical discovery. Meanwhile, nationalism was rearing its head. Devotion to the nation replaced devotion to God. Europe was torn apart by war. Sadly, all this has continued. The world is fragmenting into ever smaller entities, when its overwhelming need is unity. Moreover, there has been a meteoric increase in weapons of mass destruction.

A second contributing factor to the cultural climate had been the Enlightenment. Headed by thinkers such as Descartes, Locke and Hume, this was an eighteenth-century development of Renaissance principles, and has exercised incalculable influence on subsequent attitudes. Agnostic about God, it placed human reason centre stage – reason which would unveil a universal religion shorn of Christian excrescences, and a universal morality in which everyone would seek the greatest good of the greatest number. Universal human rights were born, and the idea of the fatherhood of God was replaced by the brotherhood of man. Although we have to thank the Enlightenment for many benefits, it has helped to bring about the common conviction that this world is all that really matters, and that religion is at best empirically unverifiable and socially divisive.

A third factor that we had to take into account when engaged in evangelism was the growth of scientific materialism and its associated technology. These have ushered us into a world utterly beyond the imagination of our forebears. Although it all began with the Christian worldview of scientists who, like Bacon, believed that God had revealed himself in two books, the book of nature and the book of Scripture, science later came to espouse a largely secular worldview. Married to an Enlightenment rationalism and the principle of radical doubt, scientific materialism became a major threat to Christian teaching, as this was popularly conceived. Though Newton was a believer, his follower Laplace famously replied to the Emperor Napoleon, when rebuked about the absence of God in his scheme of the universe, 'Sire, I have no need of that hypothesis.' Darwin's theory of evolution provided an alternative to divine creation, which was rapidly seized on by the sciences. Marx and Freud, though not strictly scientists, had a decisive effect on the twentieth-century abandonment of God. Instead of Christianity's promised kingdom of God, Marx offered the idea of a class struggle, eventually leading to an economic and social utopia. Freud undercut the whole religious worldview by regarding it as illusory, a purely psychological phenomenon.

These were some of the factors, along with increased urbanization and the experience of horrific suffering in two devastating world wars, which helped to create the climate in which I was reared and trained to preach the gospel. It was the age of Modernism, and, without serious distortion, one could say that it held six basic beliefs.

First, belief in humankind: we, not God, are in charge of our world and destiny. Second, belief in science: this will provide the key to all knowledge and advance. Third, belief in progress: we are evolving towards a better future at all levels. Fourth, belief in facts, empirically verified, as the only path to truth: values, including faith, are anyone's choice. Fifth, belief in freedom: especially from church, dogma and empire. And finally, belief in human goodness: away with dour talk of sin – we all have hearts of gold.

As evangelists, therefore, we tended to employ arguments for the existence of God and the possibility of miracles, and we encouraged scepticism about universal progress and the unblemished goodness of human nature. Though we did not realize it, we ourselves were part of the Enlightenment, a rationalist culture which we deplored. Our effectiveness was severely limited.

But what we, or at any rate I, failed to understand in the 1950s and early 1960s was that 'the times they are a-changin''. We did not realize at the time that we were part of a major culture shift, as significant as that from the Bronze to the Iron Age, or from the Middle Ages to the Renaissance. As the British Chief Rabbi Jonathan Sachs put it, 'The old era is dying: the new is waiting to be born.'

Postmodernism
The birth of the new era did not come about as a result of Christian influence. It dawned as people began to see that the picture painted by Modernism was ludicrously optimistic. We were destroying the environment: the ozone layer, the seas, the rainforests and the land itself. We possessed the capacity to

destroy the world in a nuclear holocaust, and this risk increased as more nations joined the nuclear club. We were ravaged by AIDS, the most potent scourge since the Black Death. We were witnessing the increasing breakdown of community, as individualism and violence took charge. Claiming to be free, men and women were increasingly obviously in chains of different sorts. The myths of the essential goodness of human nature and the inevitability of progress had worn remarkably thin, especially in the light of two world wars and the Holocaust.

The whole package derived from the Age of Reason had become suspect. And since the 1960s, it has been decisively rejected. What has emerged is 'postmodernism'. Nobody knows quite what to call it, but it is 'post' the Modernism that had dominated Europe for two hundred years. That world-view had outlived its shelf life. It is one thing to replace God by reason, which is what happened when Modernism replaced Christendom. It is a very different matter to replace reason when reason fails. But we can no longer believe that reason undergirds all knowledge. Darwin's theory of natural selection, Freud's psychological explorations and Marx's economic theory have not left reason unscathed as queen of the intellectual world. After all, our loves, our hates and our feelings are not grounded in reason alone! There is no longer any generally accepted big story of the world, be it God or reason, which accounts for everything, no 'meta-story'. That accounts for the existential despair among many thoughtful people. We are just left with our own little stories. In the absence of any universally accepted framework, you had better make your own choices, and nobody has the right to question them

– since there is no ultimate standard. Choice is the key to it all, in the supermarket both of food and of ideas.

Because of this depressing lack of any overarching framework with which to make sense of the world, we are left very much on our own. An *anomie* prevails, which leads to many of the characteristics of postmodernism, a worldview which is difficult to describe but the features of which we all encounter every day.

There is, first and foremost, the denial of all absolutes in truths or morality (despite the logical fallacy which that denial of absolutes involves!). There is distrust of authority figures – after all, they just represent Nietzsche's 'will to power'. There is also a general cynicism about institutions: the law, the government and the church, for example. There are few or no moral norms, except perhaps disapproval of paedophilia and approval of ecology, though neither of these is sacrosanct. There is a good deal of scorn for the past, and loss of hope in the future. The result? Live for self, and don't bother about other people. Live for now, buy on the never-never, and don't worry about the future. Written communication increasingly gives way to digital and visual, while linear thinking and even logical consistency are at a discount. It is the age of the soundbite and the photo call, the age of no foundations. Our feelings matter just as much as our reason, and much more than our history. And yet, curiously, this is an age which is spiritually hungry. At a time when church attendance is in almost universal decline in the West, except for parts of the United States, the hunger for spirituality is exploding. It is not a search for Christianity any more. Many do not think that Christianity has much spirituality. It is much more a search for fullness of life and

experience, by people who have tasted all the fruits of materialism and found them wanting. 'There must be more to life
than this,' they say. This accounts for the fascination with new
cults, the recourse to Eastern religions, spiritualism or New
Age mysticism, Wicca and bizarre sexual experimentation.
Anything to fill that persistent sense of emptiness which so
many people feel.

Towards a new approach
Given this climate, two things are obvious. First, nobody is
finding evangelism easy. The Catholics find it difficult because
they are essentially a hierarchical institution, and hierarchy is
very unattractive to postmoderns. The evangelicals find it
difficult, both because of their insistence on the reliability of
the Scriptures written more than two thousand years ago, and
because of their dogma regarding the necessity for repentance
and faith. The latter provokes the question: 'Who is going to
tell me what to do? I accept no authority but my own.' The
liberal strand in Christianity also finds it difficult. It depends
very much on the reasonableness of the Christian faith, and
nowadays intellectual argument leaves people cold. It smells
of a discarded rationalism. Perhaps the charismatics are best
placed to speak to today's postmoderns, with their emphasis
on experience of the Holy Spirit, which connects with the
widespread spiritual search for experience. Yet it is easy to
discount them too, in a day when everyone values their
own experience and believes little that they have not themselves experienced.

The other thing that is obvious is that there must be a radical
reappraisal of evangelistic approaches. It is no good mounting

rationalistic arguments in a non-rationalistic age. Giving five reasons for the existence of God is not going to cut any ice among people who want to experience for themselves whether or not there is a God. People who assume that all religions are much the same will not be greatly impressed by arguments about the supremacy of Jesus: they will be impressed when they see a radical change of life, or healing in a friend as a result of commitment to Jesus. Postmoderns are not going to be impressed by multiple arguments for the resurrection. They will cheerfully concede it, and add, 'Sure, Jesus probably rose from the dead, but so did Elvis!' We have to take a new tack.

But it will not be easy. As early as the 1940s, Arnold Toynbee saw very clearly the dangers which beset a society that no longer had an accepted moral framework. He studied twenty-one civilizations, from Babylon to the Aztecs. In every case, their collapse was not due primarily to attack from without, but to corruption from within. Cultural suicide was the problem. He saw the following as signs of a disintegrating society.

Licence replaces creativity. Escapism grows, in the cult of entertainment. People accept drift, a meaningless determinism, as if our efforts cannot make any difference. There is noticeable self-loathing, arising from moral abandon. And promiscuity increases, not only in the sexual area, but in an unfocused eclecticism and an uncritical tolerance, together with a surrender to the 'mass mind' in religion, literature, journalism and art.

These are some of the consequences when faith in the transcendent is abandoned. And that is what is happening today. There is (probably – so say the atheists, just to be on the safe side!) no God. There are no absolutes. Truth claims are an attempt at power and must be resisted. The most dangerous people are those who are convinced they are right. The 'modern' world must be dismantled – this was very clear in the 1960s with hippy culture, sexual revolution, abortion, anti-Vietnam war protests and so forth. It is no less clear today.

The results are hardly reassuring. We have a massive increase in violence, the selfishness of the 'Me' generation, the collapse of the family, the escalation of divorce, widespread abortion, and sexual experimentation even among pre-teens. Nothing is 'wrong'. It is just 'not my preference'. This is all part of the deconstruction which postmodernism advocates. This world is all there is. Whoever has the most toys wins. Hence, the massive growth of shopping malls, today's cathedrals to Mammon. Hence, too, the materialism and consumerism that corrodes the West. We have no identity, other than the multiple parts we play. So fashion matters. Show matters – we need our Jaguars to show how important we are. Style matters more than substance.

It is the group that sets the trends: the yuppies, Generations X and Y. People define themselves in terms of gender, race, sexual preference, class, or names like 'environmentalists', 'animal rights activists', 'organic food devotees' and the like. But many know it is a dead end. They are disenchanted. Fashions change, friends leave, fear grows. Will anyone like me? Can I find – or keep – a mate? Increasingly we are witnessing serial polygamy, as people frantically search for 'love'. Individuals are all too often locked in mutually inaccessible worlds. Postmodernism stresses tolerance, multiculturalism, pluralism, but denies all beliefs, trivializes all cultures and becomes ever more intolerant of those who do not toe the politically correct line. Today we are seeing, in this postmodern society, the emptiness of living without God.

Evangelism – some fresh trends

None of us knows all the answers of how to speak into this culture. But I am finding some contemporary trends useful.

1. First, there has been the shift from the **crusade model** (so effective in the mid-twentieth century) to the **local church**. It is partly that people are not keen to go along to hear any speaker pontificate nowadays, unless that speaker is widely trusted, such as Franklin Graham in the US or J.John in the UK. Instead, the local church, when it is alive and prepared to put itself out in mission, is much more likely than a crusade to win new converts these days. It can have a sustained influence on its locality, and people can assess its credibility, lifestyle, leadership and message. The visiting speaker and his or her entourage are much more suspect. What are they like when they are at home? Are they making money out of this venture? Are they *real*? After all, Jesus did not leave us a crusade, but a church!

2. There is a second very marked trend: from **crisis** to **process**. When I was young, most English people believed in God and in Jesus – they simply were not connected up. The job of the evangelist was to help them make that connection, and one of the common methods was to call people to the front after an evangelistic address at church, to indicate their decisive response to Christ. Today most people are much further back. They are not at all sure about God. Many know almost nothing about Jesus. To call for an immediate response would be both counterproductive and countercultural. People today want to look before they leap. And so most effective

evangelism now takes place in short courses, such as Alpha, Christianity Explored and the Start Course. These encourage exploration into the faith, within a warm context, and without pressure. Thus, they allow participants to respond in their own time, rather than in that of the evangelist. It is a big change, and an important one.

3. A third trend I have noticed is from **technique** to **relationship**. In my early days in evangelism, there was a lot of emphasis on technique: the evangelistic booklet, the four spiritual laws, the ABC of commitment, and so on. Today that has vanished so completely that we have gone to the other extreme, and many established Christians have no clear idea of how they can help their friends to faith. Relationship is all-important. It is sometimes called friendship evangelism, though there is often lots of friendship and little evangelism – for fear that the relationship may be spoiled. But in an age when words are suspect, it is our friendships that give us the right to speak about the things that really matter. Friendship is crucial.

4. Evangelists tend to want to **talk** a lot, and get their message over at all costs, whether people want to hear it or not. (I know I used to be like that!) But nowadays I remember that I have two ears and one mouth. I need to do a lot of **listening**: partly because that is a good way to get to know someone, since people love talking about themselves; and partly because in this postmodern world people come from such diverse backgrounds that we need to listen carefully if we are going to be able to speak effectively to their condition.

5. Another change is from **indiscriminate** to **focused** outreach. I know I used to be happy to give much the same message in any gathering, however it was made up and whatever

the age range. But not now. Appropriate approaches are needed for the different groups we are called to relate to. We would adopt a very different style and vocabulary when addressing respectively a dinner party, a student meeting, a debate, a church service and a youth gathering. The message might be much the same, but the way it is presented differs widely.

6. Most of us now find that the **church building** is not the best place in which to proclaim the gospel. It used to be, but no longer. One way and another, people either have been hurt by the church or have simply never been in one. 'Church' carries all sorts of negative associations. Many people are as unwilling to enter a church building as I am to go into a Mormon temple. It is alien, not part of my scene. So lots of people will not come if they are invited to a church presentation. And if they do come, they will probably feel uncomfortable. So it is important not to urge them (in vain) to come to our turf, but rather to go to theirs. The home, the pub, the leisure centre, the town hall, the lecture room, or wherever those we are seeking to help feel most at home – that is where we need to be. Ironically, the church building has become the very worst place in which to try to win people for Christ.

7. If you listen to a skilled evangelist these days, you may notice a distinct shift in the content of the message, from what it would have been some years ago. It is still Christ-centred and biblical, but there is less emphasis on **doctrines** that have to be believed, than on meeting **spiritual needs** of which people are aware. There is more of an emphasis on the whole person rather than just a soul to be saved. There is more listening to the cries of the heart, the interests and acknowledged needs of the community, than simply delivering a message from the

Bible. Do not mistake what I am saying, for all good evangelism is biblically based, but today it is more nuanced to the sense of emptiness and hunger for spirituality which so many post-modern people have. I sometimes do a talk: 'In search of spirituality', and it tends to draw a crowd.

8. There is a corresponding shift from emphasizing **truth** to responding to people's **deep concerns**. Many folk have little clear concept of truth these days. They say, 'It may be true for you, but it is not true for me.' They may think that truth claims are your attempt to gain power over them and make them think your way. Of course, you know that the gospel is true, but they don't, so it is best to find another way into their hearts. People today are concerned about identity: who am I when the masks are off? They are concerned about value: what am I worth when I can be sacked at any time, or my family can desert me? They are concerned about purpose: what is the point of life? Just to exist, or is there some bigger purpose that I may be missing? What about right and wrong: are they just social conventions? What about death: is it the end or not? What does it mean to be human, when we can create the starter kit for life in the laboratory? The gospel speaks directly to such questions, and I have found them a marvellous starting point in explaining the good news in a way that makes real sense to people. But I would not have started in this way thirty years ago!

9. There are other changes I have noticed, too. There is a shift from **declaration** to **celebration**. Of course, we still declare what God has done in Christ, but we gain people's attention much more readily if they can see the sheer joy, the celebration in the Christian community. It raises the question

in their hearts: 'What have these people got to be so excited about?' That was the reaction when we did Israeli circle dancing in a main street, and again in a motorway car park – sheer celebration by students we had taken away on a mission. It immediately drew a crowd, in a way someone just getting up and speaking would not have done. A five-minute talk in a barn dance is worth many a half-hour sermon! Everyone loves a party, but sadly many people are quite ignorant of the good news that gives us such cause for celebration. We need to let it hang out!

10. There is another most welcome change. In the eighteenth- and nineteenth-century revivals of Christianity, there was strong **social concern**: for the poor, the marginalized, the oppressed. But early in the twentieth century that changed, and churches tended to divide. The conservative ones majored on preaching the gospel of salvation. The more liberal ones concentrated on caring for the needs of society. That was a stupid dichotomy among followers of Jesus, who after all went about doing good *and* preaching the kingdom of God! Happily, it is widely recognized now that we have to match our proclamation of God's loving care with our actions. This is particularly important in a society which is casual about promises and cynical about words, particularly the words of politicians and preachers. A lot of effective evangelism today is the fruit of much practical care in meeting human need. And so it should be.

11. Thirty years ago, I think I would have seen public evangelism as the province of a single person, a clergyman or some other competent speaker. Now I see it much more as an overflowing community event, run by a **team**. They give

the (true) impression that the spreading of the good news cannot be left to the professionals, but is the function of all Christians, in one way or another.

Last Sunday I went to my church, which had just run a fabulous holiday club for large numbers of children, who in turn dragged their parents along on the Sunday. I found myself sitting next to someone whose small daughter had been invited by one of her friends, and had enjoyed it so much that she pestered her mother to come. This was the woman's first time in the church, and she could hardly contain herself. The involvement of the teenagers, the fun, the humour, the songs, the sheer energy and the variety of people taking leading parts, all left her breathless. She had never seen anything like it in her life. I am sure she will be back. Evangelism is the function of a community overflowing with joy and energy, not simply of a single preacher.

Thankfully, there is much more of that sort of thing in evangelistic events these days. Good preaching has a central place, but so too does powerful worship, drama, testimony, videos and an atmosphere of warmth and discovery. It arouses the curiosity. It draws people back. It is a valuable shift from bald preaching in church by a single evangelist, such as we would have experienced a few decades ago.

12. Finally, there is another change that I welcome. It is a shift from each church paddling its own canoe independently of other churches, to **partnership**. Some years ago, I went to encourage the ministers of about 1,800 churches in Atlanta, Georgia. Despite their differences, they had all banded together in preparation for the Olympics. Next week I am going to speak to Christians from diverse churches in a small town

which are pulling together to run several Alpha courses. This sense of partnership now runs right across the denominations, which it certainly would not have done a few decades ago.

Why, I remember being reported to the Archbishop of Canterbury by a Welsh bishop because I was leading a mission in Wales which involved non-conformist churches. The Archbishop had the good sense to encourage me to continue! Mercifully, you don't find much of that separatist and isolationist attitude these days. The good news is so good that it needs all types of church and denominations which profess the New Testament faith to proclaim its essentials with joy and partnership. Then there is some hope of people believing it. But as long as they see the unloving divisions of the church, they can rightly say, 'If this lot can't agree between themselves, they certainly won't find me joining them. I have enough troubles of my own!'

Bishop Lesslie Newbigin's wisdom

These are some of the changes that have come about during the past thirty years or more, particularly in the evangelistic response to postmodernism. But of course they are not enough. Perhaps that great Christian leader, the late Bishop Lesslie Newbigin, can help us at this point. After his return from much of a lifetime spent as a missionary in India, he found the apathy and materialistic secularism of postmodern England even harder to penetrate than the Hinduism with which he had engaged for so long. He wrote, lectured and preached tirelessly, and I had the privilege of knowing him quite well.

He recognized the force of postmodernism's reaction against power structures in our society. Royalty, government, police, teachers, parents and the church have all at times been oppressive and domineering. The church, he acknowledged, has rightly earned censure for its moralism, its zealous repudiation or suppression of other worldviews in the course of its missionary advance, and at times its attitudes to science, sexuality and freedom.

Newbigin recognized that one of the great concerns of postmodernism is the hunger for community, not community in some vague, idealistic form, but tight-knit communities of people, with shared characteristics or common interests, such as black people, gays, teenagers and so forth. The church must become the community radiating an unjudging welcome to one and all, just as Jesus welcomed all, before he set to work to transform them.

But Newbigin was concerned by the rootlessness and instability of the postmodern scene, with its divorce from history and traditional understanding of life and values. This leaves many people unable to cope with the stresses and insecurities of life, and so they pin their hopes on tarot cards, horoscopes and the lottery. Accordingly, he strongly stressed the historical nature of the Christian faith. It is not an ideology or a philosophy. Christianity bears witness to something God has done in the historic coming, dying and rising of Jesus Christ.

This led him to his main contention, that in this age, which is so sceptical of meta-narrative, we have a story, the most wonderful story in the world, of the interaction of God with humankind: a story that is trustworthy, a story in which we are personally involved, a story open to all who will enter it. We also have another story, of what the Lord has done in our own lives. We cannot prove our case, but we can witness to it, with life and lip. The lack of confident Christian witness is perhaps the greatest weakness of the contemporary church, and yet this could be the greatest way for the gospel to spread.

Lesslie Newbigin is the best apologist that Christianity has thrown up since the arrival of postmodernism, and we shall certainly need good apologetics if the gospel is to commend itself. But Newbigin knew that, while some are called to intellectual defence of the faith, it is not everyone's gift. What does, however, lie within the capability of every Christian is the ability to live an attractive life, transformed by Jesus Christ, a confidence in the great, historically reliable story of the faith, a willingness to be joyful and fearless in bearing witness to Christ's impact on our lives, and membership of a Christian community which lives out that faith in love and welcome to those who are still strangers to the love of God.

Chapter 9

REASON TO BELIEVE

In the previous chapter I have shown some of the ways in which Christian evangelism has altered over my lifetime, and have hinted at a few of the changed emphases that are evident in gospel preaching today. Now I want to point to two important developments: one of them good, and one not so good.

The growth of apologetics
Perhaps the obscure and somewhat cumbersome word 'apologetics' needs some explanation. It does not mean saying 'Sorry', nor does it mean being apologetic about the message we proclaim. The word (and there does not seem to be an adequate replacement) comes from the Greek. The noun means 'a defence' or 'a reason for believing something', while the verb means 'to give a reason' and it is famously used in 1 Peter 3:15–17, where Christians are urged to be 'prepared to give an answer to everyone who asks you to give the reason for the hope that you have'. They are not to be frightened of doing it, but are to do it with gentleness and respect. They must set

Christ apart as Lord in their lives, if they want to be effective. They are to keep their conscience clear. And they are to be prepared, if necessary, to suffer for their faith. That is a good description of Christian apologetics. It is no mere rehearsing of academic arguments, but the answer from a warm heart, a clear conscience, a Christ-centred life and an informed mind to those who want to know why we are Christians. It is something so central to our faith that we must be prepared to suffer for it.

Over the past thirty years or so, I have seen a significant growth in apologetics in the ministry of the best evangelists. It will not do simply to shout louder when people oppose or neglect what we have to say. It will not do to say, 'I preach the simple gospel.' The gospel is like the sea, where a child can paddle, but so deep too that a giraffe will soon be out of its depth! If we are to serve our generation aright, it is incumbent on preachers of the gospel to know, and when appropriate explain, the solid reasons which validate faith. You can never argue anyone into the kingdom of God. But you can show that commitment to Christ is not lunacy or mere emotionalism. It does not require you to throw away your God-given reason. Revelation, not reason, is the king, but reason is the prime minister.

So how does all this relate to evangelism, you may wonder? Professor Alister McGrath explains with admirable lucidity:

A rough working definition of evangelism might be 'inviting someone to become a Christian'. Apologetics would then be 'clearing the ground for that invitation so that it is more likely to receive a positive response'. Apologetics shows the

reasonableness and attractiveness of the Christian faith.
Evangelism is encouraging someone to take the step for which
apologetics has prepared the way.[1]

In a word, apologetics aims to bring understanding, evangelism
to offer challenge.

Why should apologetics figure more prominently in today's
evangelistic addresses? Partly because so many people are
entirely ignorant about the faith, and need to be informed
before any challenge is made. And partly because what we
assumed a few decades ago can no longer be taken for granted.
We took for granted the existence of God. We took for granted
an objective moral code. We took for granted the historicity
and deity of Jesus Christ. We took for granted that Christianity
was the best and greatest of world faiths. Now all these assumptions are widely dismissed or at least radically questioned.

Many people imagine that Christianity is a fairy tale, like
Father Christmas. Others think it has been swept away by the
advance of science. Others think it is just a matter of being
nice to people. But all of these notions are far from the truth.
Jesus was a historical figure, as well attested as Julius Caesar.
He was so significant that all history is dated before or after
him. His resurrection is acclaimed by leading ancient historians
as one of the best-attested facts in Roman history. He is alive
today, and able to transform the lives of those who get
connected to him. We can be quite unashamed about this
central issue in the Christian faith. Apologetics seeks both to
show the solidity of the Christian evidences, and also to repulse
the attacks which are constantly being made against the faith.
Thus, apologetics has both a positive aspect, commending

Christianity, and a defensive aspect, contending against world-views which deny or relativize Christ. Apologetics is like a bulldozer clearing the rocks out of the way on the road to Christ, and repairing that road so that travellers can go down it. Evangelism is like taking a friend with us down that road until they are ready for an introduction to Jesus himself. The apologetic enterprise is not a rationalistic occupation for eggheads. It is not an attempt to argue anyone into the faith, as if that were possible. Apologetics and evangelism belong together. Apologetics glides into evangelism.

Apologetics in the evangelistic address

An evangelistic sermon is not normally the place for an extended intellectual defence of the faith. But if it is to be effective, an evangelistic sermon must engage with the assumptions that hearers are likely to bring with them. These may come either from deeply held beliefs, or from some topical issue which is currently on everyone's minds.

For example, if I were giving an evangelistic talk in Britain today, 5 September 2010, I would feel almost bound to refer to the confident assertion three days earlier by the distinguished physicist Stephen Hawking that, when considering the origin of the universe, God is an unnecessary hypothesis. Once an agnostic churchgoer, Professor Hawking appears to have just gone public as an atheist. He maintains that the laws of physics, not the will of God, suffice to explain the existence of life on this planet. The Big Bang, he believes, which started it all off, was the inevitable consequence of these laws. But how could I respond to this, without getting bogged down in it, and ruining the thrust of my address?

I would realize that this sort of claim, enthusiastically taken up in the media, is attractive to the modern sceptic, especially when it appears as the main headline in the London *Times*. It would reinforce the disinclination of my hearers to take Christianity seriously. So my evangelistic talk would fall on deaf ears, if I did not at least allude to an assumption which would invalidate all I have to say. Accordingly, I might quote a sentence from Hawking: 'Because there is a law such as gravity, the universe can and will create itself from nothing.'[2] I might point out, in response, that physical laws do not create anything: they are merely a description of observed uniformities. So it is ridiculous to claim that gravity creates the universe.

Alternatively, I might ask how gravity came to exist in the first place. What agency, if not God, put it there? How come that it possesses such remarkable properties? As Professor John Lennox robustly replied in another newspaper, Hawking appears to confuse law with agency. His invitation to us to choose between God and physical laws is as mistaken as it would be to invite the same choice between Sir Frank Whittle and the laws of physics to explain the origin of the jet engine![3] The succinct and rather humorous way in which John Lennox makes his point is infused with a powerful logic and a lucid clarity. It clarifies the situation, with an economy of language and an unanswerable logic that is precisely what you want to use in a sermon that is not primarily about the existence of God at all.

Or else I might point out that if human beings spring from no intelligent Creator, then inevitably we are nothing more than a collection of random molecules, the end product of a mindless process. If that were the case, then it would undermine the very rationality we need to study science. Our conclusions would be as meaningless as the world in which we live. And that would include Stephen Hawking's assertion!

There are other ways of handling it. I could point out that we are moral beings, who know the difference between right and wrong. But there is no scientific route to establishing ethics. Or I might draw attention to the religious tradition of humankind – practically the whole of the human race throughout its history has believed in a Creator God. That is no proof, of course, but it does raise a presumption which cannot be banished merely by a powerful headline from a distinguished scientist. Or I could observe, as Dr Lennox does, that when we see letters which form our name scratched in the sand, we recognize that a human agent must have done it. How much stronger is the argument when the DNA database of humanity runs to 3.5 billion 'letters'! That was enough to lead Francis Collins, head of the Human Genome Project, to Christian belief. He simply could not believe it was an accident.

A defence of this sort does not need to be extended. Its value is to puncture the easy-going acceptance of an anti-God statement by a famous man. It deals briefly but usefully with a current topic which would make acceptance of the gospel difficult. It shows that there is another side to the argument. Indeed, it undermines the presuppositions that lie behind the anti-God assertion. And in so doing, it may well open the minds of the hearers to the main thrust of what you want to say.

Or suppose you are preaching evangelistically about Jesus, maybe at Christmas time. Inevitably, some of your hearers will imagine that it is just a lovely story, but not to be taken as factual, any more than Santa or the little green men at the bottom of the garden. It would be wise to face this assumption early in your address, and to point out succinctly that the existence of Jesus of Nazareth is more certain than that of any other ancient figure.

His teaching was more than merely human: nobody had ever heard anything to match it for profundity, clarity, breadth of appeal and authority. His influence was greater than that of any warrior, ruler or philosopher. It touched all kinds of people, and still does, at the rate of many thousands a day. His behaviour was impeccable. He had all the virtues known to men and women, and none of the vices. The ideal for human life is not beyond us. It has been embodied in Jesus. His fulfilment of prophecy was unique. His conception, birthplace, teaching in parables, triumphal entry into Jerusalem, his suffering, his shameful death, his burial in a rich man's tomb, and his ultimate vindication through the resurrection – all these were predicted in Scripture, centuries beforehand. And they all came to pass in this one man's life. That is unparalleled in human history. You could point out how his miracles powerfully support his claims: they were acted parables, never to show off, always to help or heal, or else to point in a graphic way to himself and what he could do for people. His claims, to forgive sins, to accept worship, to be the final judge of all, certainly persuaded his disciples, as they have persuaded millions since. He himself said that his death would be a ransom for many who put their trust in him, and, as a result, the largest religion the world has ever seen came into being. Countless millions of men, women and children have discovered a new dimension to life by their trust in what that death achieved for them. Finally, you could point to his resurrection, the most powerful demonstration of his claims, and one of the best-attested facts in ancient history.

This can be done speedily. It need not take up more than three minutes or so of your address. But it will ensure that people listen with fresh attention to what follows. Of course, you need to be able to back up any of your assertions, but the place for that is not in the pulpit, but beforehand in the study. Your aim is to draw people to the authentic Jesus, but part of your method is to validate his authenticity.

Perhaps you plan to preach evangelistically on the common question: 'What makes Jesus so special?' In today's climate of religious pluralism, your purpose will not be to denigrate other faiths, but to show the unique splendour of Jesus, before which all other faiths pale into insignificance. You could point out that no other great religious leader ever claimed to bring God to the stage of human history, and to embody all of the divine that could be contained within a human frame. No other great religious teacher ever dealt in a radical way with the persistent tide of human wickedness: but Jesus, the God-man, took personal responsibility for it on the cross, and was thus empowered to offer forgiveness to all who come to him in repentance and faith. You could go on to show that no other great religious teacher ever rose from the grave, and you could either show the evidence for that confidence, or contrast it with other great religious figures who remain securely in their tombs. You could show the fourth great mark of Christ's superiority and uniqueness by pointing out that, alone among the religious leaders of the world, he offers to come by his unseen, but very real, Spirit into the hearts of men and women, with transforming power. In giving such a fourfold presentation of the uniqueness of Jesus, you could contrast him with the leaders of other faiths, their lives and teachings, as much or as little as you wished.

And emphasis on the ability of Jesus to come and share the lives of those who trust him leads very naturally to the evangelist's challenge for his hearers to take the step of surrendering to this unique Saviour. I remember taking just this approach among a group of young graduates, who were initially unimpressed by the Christian faith or hostile to it. A number of them came that day to an understanding of the uniqueness of Jesus, and then entrusted their lives to him. The apologetics had fed into the evangelism.

There are not a great many common objections to the Christian faith. The same ones turn up all the time, and you could rehearse them on the fingers of two hands. But it is important for the evangelist in today's pluralist, sceptical and multinational society to have thought deeply about those objections. He or she needs to be able to produce a response, which may be shorter or longer, according to circumstances.

Apologetics as the primary evangelistic instrument

I have suggested that, generally, our apologetic material will be an important, but comparatively small, part of the evangelistic talk. There are times, however, when apologetics takes over and prepares the ground, both in the head and the heart, for a short but carefully planned appeal at the end. I have found that to be the case when treating subjects such as 'What does it mean to be human?', 'Christian confidence in an age of pluralism', 'Is truth relative?', 'Values in a shifting society' or 'Has life any ultimate meaning?'.

Basically, what is important is for preachers to be so aware of the currents of thought, assumptions and problems which affect their hearers, as well as knowing the major interests of the media, that they are able to use them as channels through which the truth of God can find its entrance into hearts and minds. There will be times when people need to go away with a very clear understanding of how God has acted to meet us in our suffering, how he can accept us when we are unacceptable, how we can be confident that he exists, and why we are quietly confident of life after death. These are vital issues. They affect everyone. The preacher may not have much influence outside his or her congregation – but the congregation certainly will. Every Monday sees them scattered all over the neighbourhood or beyond, at work. How powerful it is when the work of evangelization is not restricted to the preacher, but is recognized as the calling of every member of the church, when opportunity offers itself in the workplace or in leisure activities. Good evangelism with an apologetic element facilitates this spread of the basic truths of Christianity by lay people in their normal situations.

Apologetics as a magnet

It is a mistake to think that apologetics is necessarily a defensive tool. It is also very effective in making clear the attractiveness of the gospel. Many people think that Christianity is irrelevant to them. It conjures up memory of cold churches, antiquated robes and dreary sermons. It seems to be dull and life-denying. Apologetics can make a real difference to this attitude and help people to discover the sheer attractiveness of the gospel. We do not need to *make* the good news attractive. It *is* attractive.

As we saw in an earlier chapter, Jesus is the most winsome person who ever lived. But people, by and large, do not realize this. And apologetics is a sensible way of showing the attractiveness of Jesus. What I have in mind is the presenting of the Christian faith in an intriguing way on neutral ground. It may be a debate in a town hall or university lecture theatre. It may be an impromptu gathering at a funeral wake or in a home discussion group.

I recall going to visit someone on one occasion and I found a crowd in the house – there had been a death, and friends had gathered. They asked me if I would like to view the body. I replied that I would much rather spend time with them, and I spoke of Jesus' resurrection as the sure ground for Christian hope after death. They were fascinated. They realized, perhaps for the first time, that the Christian faith was relevant to the situation they were in, and that it was very attractive indeed, especially when there was no other ground for hope. I remember speaking in a large room in Cape Town, packed with students, on the subject 'Choose freedom'. This was in the apartheid era, when freedom was an extremely live issue. People were ecstatic when they appreciated the liberation Jesus could bring, not just racially, but from the hatred and bitterness that corrode the heart.

It is a question of discerning the prevalent issues that are occupying people's minds, and then preparing a talk that engages with them, and shows something of the joy and peace and fulfilment that Christ can offer.

I remember speaking not long ago in a home in the United States on the subject: 'Can we have peace in a world plagued by terror?' It certainly drew people. And in addition to giving solid reasons, I gave examples from three men of God who demonstrated peace most wonderfully in the midst of terror, because of their relationship with Jesus. It was easy from that point to commend Jesus to those present. Several came to trust him that day, and a small nurture group emerged.

Jesus said, 'I have come that they may have life, and have it to the full' (John 10:10). You could not have any more attractive claim than that. It is up to us to pass it on with intelligence, warmth and conviction. Sadly, the church has not always been characterized by that 'fullness of life' which Jesus offered.

Apologetics in the open air

Open-air proclamation of the gospel has a noble history, reaching back through Wesley and Whitefield, Francis of Assisi, Gregory, Irenaeus and Justin, to Jesus and his apostles. It is big business in Africa, but it has fallen into disrepute in the West these days. You will tell me that it has had its day. But this is not the case. The old-fashioned form of open-air meeting is a thing of the past, with a dreary-looking person on a street corner, urging all and sundry to prepare for the judgment of God. But that is not the only way of proclaiming the good news in the open air. It can be done, for instance, by using a simple questionnaire. When a baptism or even a Communion service is carried out in a public area, I have found that the opportunities for discussion afterwards with interested passers-by are considerable.

But the most obvious sort of open-air work is when a church or student group goes to a well-populated place and draws a crowd through music, drama, dance, clowning or the like. In between the various items, someone can explain succinctly in the most down-to-earth language the wonder of God's love and the need to make a response. If you try this, you will see the two sides of apologetics. The short talks and personal testimonies can show the attractiveness of the gospel, and so too do the joyful conversations which helpers have with those in the crowd. But you will need all the defensive armour that apologetics can supply, because you will be assailed from all sides with objections, ridicule, anger and interest. You will learn the questions that are on people's hearts. You will learn to distinguish real issues from smokescreens, designed to keep you at arm's length. You will discover the agenda for a truly relevant apologetic as the handmaid for evangelism. You will draw some people to Christ. And you will show that the Christian community is not embarrassed to come out of its safe ground in church buildings, but has a message designed for everybody, and a confidence to make it known. I have found open-air ministry like this to be some of the most rewarding – and challenging – evangelism I have ever done.

The decline of eschatology

Eschatology means 'the last things'. The term is usually applied to the final arrival of the kingdom of God, but it is also used of the end of human life, and the question of what, if anything, follows it. It is in this sense that I want to use the term as we consider its place in evangelism.

In Victorian days, the appeal of heaven and the fear of hell were commonplace in evangelism. They were probably over-emphasized, because, although they figure in the teaching of the New Testament, they could easily be misused to bring people to a Christian profession for the sake of what they could gain by it, or for the sake of escaping a horrible alternative. And true evangelism does not major on rewards or punishment, but on the person and achievement of Jesus and the powerful attraction he exerts. Nevertheless, when every allowance is made for the dangers of misuse, the almost complete disappearance of heaven and hell from the content of much of today's evangelism is remarkable. What can account for it?

It may be partly due to a reaction against overemphasis on the subject in Victorian days. But that is not an adequate reason. I believe that evangelists today have surrendered, perhaps without knowing it, to the secular assumption that this world is all there is, and this life is the only one we have. That view is rife in our culture. And it is novel.

The whole thrust of Egyptian religion was towards the afterlife and how to thrive in it: that is why the tombs of the powerful were equipped with all the goods they would need in that afterlife. Greek and Roman religion was likewise fairly clear that there would be life after death. So was Christendom for many centuries. So is Islam. So are most of the religions in the world.

The striking exception is the secularized West. For as our standards of living have increased, so too has our concentration on getting all we can from this life. Materialism is the curse of the West, and our concern is all for money and what it can buy. That is of course very selfish. It is also dangerous, because there remains no ultimate sanction against a Hitler or a Pol Pot. There is no hell to await them. They do not get punished for their unspeakable atrocities. You are allowed to make no moral differentiation between Stalin and Mother Teresa, since there are no objective values. The two have simply made different choices. This is one of the most disastrous conclusions of postmodernism.

In unthinking conformity with this novel assumption that nothing awaits us after death, Christianity has become very horizontal, and this-worldly. Little is heard of the Christian hope and its counterpart, even among evangelists. But if we neglect the last things, we remove an important part of the gospel.

Every worldview has a future goal to which it strives. Think of communism, with its struggle towards the fulfilment state. Think of utilitarianism, driven by the quest for the greatest good of the greatest number. Think of the Muslim zeal for paradise – so strong that men and women are prepared to blow themselves up, so long as they are thereby killing their enemies in war, and thus being assured of the joys of paradise.

Christianity, too, has a future destiny toward which it moves. The teaching of Jesus was constantly concerned with it, as he came proclaiming the kingdom of heaven. He often spoke with joy and assurance about the blessing of heaven, the future part of that kingdom of God, which he had come to inaugurate. He spoke with frequency and awesome clarity about the danger of hell for those who decisively turned their backs on God. He declared that he had come into this world for judgment. He was the light of the world, which would either attract you or else you would shrink away from it, further into the darkness.

The point is that we have been given free will. We are as free as the fresher going up to university, the architect taking a briefing from his employer and going away to make his plans, or the banker making up his mind what futures to invest in. Free. But we are also accountable. And accountability is always the flip side of freedom. The student will have to face the scrutiny of the examiner at her finals. The architect will have to bring his plans for acceptance or rejection. The banker may make a pile or go bust. There is always a day of judgment. And, by and large, we get what we deserve. We remain essentially self-determined, despite the fact that we are often assessed by someone else. We go to our own place.

That is true in ordinary life, and it is true in Christianity. Unless this world is an undesigned fluke, unless life is a meaningless interlude, unless the whole idea of moral values is a chimera, we *do* believe in accountability. It is the counterpart of freedom and responsible action. We *do* believe that injustice should be brought to task, that wrong should be exposed and dealt with (at least, we believe that about the misdemeanours of other people; we are not so sure when our own are under consideration). Why then should it seem incredible that God will hold us accountable for our use of the life that he has given us? If there is such a thing as a fundamental difference between right and wrong, there must be a final judgment, a day of reckoning. Shall not the Judge of all the earth do right?

Of course our hackles rise at the idea. In our world where everything seems relative, we find it extraordinarily hard to think in terms of an absolute. We find a separation between sheep and goats, saved and lost, an extraordinarily dated, not to say threatening, conception. Our charity, as well as our cynicism, persuades us that we are all going the same way. And as for God judging us, the very idea evokes a stronger resistance than any other article in the Christian creed, for it implies that we are both finite and guilty, and neither idea is in the least agreeable. Yet the assessment by another, whether by an examiner, an employer, or God, merely underlines the judgment we have already passed on ourselves by our behaviour. Our destiny ratifies the decisions we have made on how we should spend our time, how we should behave, and what attitudes we should adopt.

Yet God's judgment is very merciful. He actually lets us decide our destiny. We may let the love of God, displayed in Jesus on the cross, break down our proud self-reliance and isolationism from God, or we may, so to speak, crucify him afresh. It is up to us. We are accountable for what we do. But of this we may be sure. We shall not be judged by any arbitrary standard, but by what it means to be truly human: and the model for that is Jesus. We shall be judged by our response to the love of God shown us in the person and work of Jesus. That will determine our final destiny. We judge ourselves by the judgment we pass on him.

God's purpose for all humankind is to be with him for ever. God does not want anyone to perish, but everyone to come to repentance (2 Peter 3:9). The night before his own death, Jesus told his friends, 'In my Father's house are many rooms; if it were not so, I would have told you. I am going there to prepare a place for you' (John 14:2). What comforting words! They have blessed the deathbed of millions. But in that same context, Jesus declares. 'I am the way and the truth and the life. No-one comes to the Father except through me' (John 14:6). If we entrust our lives to Christ, he will not scrap us at the end of our days on earth. We have tasted the first instalment of eternal life here and now; we shall taste its fullness after death. But if we say no to Jesus Christ, and determine to reject him, what can we expect? God is not going to populate his heaven with conscripts who have no desire to be in his presence. He has done everything to draw us to himself. He has erected the wide arms of the cross as a barrier to keep us from the path of self-destruction. But if we push past them, what more can he do? He will not deny us the freedom to choose our destiny, which is one of the main things that makes us human. He will reluctantly underline the choice we have made. He will honour our freedom of choice, even in the hell of our own choosing. God's judgment at the end of life will both reveal and ratify the choices we have been making throughout our lives. We shall assuredly go to our own place.

So, surely it is right for the evangelist to remind people that actions and attitudes have consequences. Eternal loss is possible. But no preacher should speak of hell without tears. It is the most awesome subject, and must be very gently handled. Nevertheless, the evangelist must warn his hearers that Jesus, the most gracious, loving person who ever lived, warned his hearers about hell. He made it very clear that there is a decision to be made, and there are consequences of that decision. He told them that we are either in the feast or outside it, we are either lost or safe, we are either on the narrow way that leads to life or the broad way that leads to destruction. We are either for him or against him. We are either the wheat that will be gathered into his barn, or the weeds that will not. Always in the teaching of Jesus, there is a choice to be made which determines the future. That is why he called on people to repent, to change direction.

Interpreters differ on whether hell involves conscious torment over lost opportunities, or the total destruction of all we have aimed for. That is God's business, not ours to be dogmatic about. But we do not need to speculate. On any showing, it is terrible. Our job is to make clear that God has provided the opportunity for all to enter his heaven after death, and that it will be the complete fulfilment of every longing we have ever had. But God will not force us there. We must decide. Will we turn to him and set our faces towards the light, or turn our backs on him and enter further into the darkness which can only end in ruin? If we are to be honest with our contemporaries, then this dichotomy, this alternative, needs to enter into our preaching from time to time. People deserve to know, from the evangelist's mouth, what Jesus taught about heaven and hell. He or she must tell them, gently but firmly, that we bear the eternal consequences of our decisions.

Chapter 10

WHATEVER HAPPENED TO SIN?

Few would deny that it is much harder to proclaim the gospel in a way that really touches human hearts these days than it was a few decades ago. Modern people, as we have already seen, are further away from any understanding of authentic Christianity, and the problem of how we can refer to sin effectively in today's culture is one we find particularly difficult. The concept of sin affronts our human self-confidence, and is increasingly felt to be meaningless in today's society. I think of the street preachers a couple of decades ago, carrying billboards on their front and back with words like these on them: 'Repent and meet your God', and 'Turn or burn'. No wonder we would cross the street if we saw something like this today, in order not to be associated with such a crude approach. I suppose the occasional person may be brought to Christ in this way, but the vast majority are put off for good and think, 'If this is Christianity, I am determined to have nothing to do with it.' Nowadays we wouldn't dream of presenting the gospel in such terms. Nevertheless, recognition of sin and repentance are an inescapable part of the gospel. How are we to go about addressing it?

In Western Christianity, during the past two or three hundred years, the first point many evangelists have tended to concentrate on has been sin, the sin from which we need to be set free. Preachers have tried to convict people of their guilt before God, and then set forth Jesus Christ as the remedy for that guilt, so that we may stand tall, fully accepted in God's presence.

In other parts of the world, however, the approach has been somewhat different. In countries dominated by the Muslim concept of shame, our human predicament has been painted in those colours, and the corresponding restoration in Christ is seen as honour, something highly regarded in Islamic lands. When preaching the gospel to animists, as found in much of Africa and Asia, the most successful approach has been to contrast the fear and bondage of evil spirits under which they labour with the liberation and hope that Christ brings.

So it would appear that we may be to a large extent prisoners of our Western culture in persisting with our emphasis on the model of guilt and grace. It is perfectly valid, but it does not usually scratch people where they are itching. Guilt only becomes an intense problem, as it did for a thousand years between Augustine and Luther, if you believe in an ethical, monotheistic God, to whom you are accountable. In that millennium most people did. Today, many have surrendered to agnosticism about God and relativism about morals. Consequently, they do not share that assumption. So to major on guilt may well not be the best place to begin.

Indeed, it is not! The gospel is not primarily about sin, but about God's loving redemption. It is not so much about human wickedness, as about God's love. It is not primarily about what we are, but about what Jesus is. Sin, human wickedness, is the dark underside of the coin. The gleaming bright side is what God is like, what he has done for us, and what he offers us. This is what the evangelist needs to make plain. Of course, that would not mean a lot if our situation was already ideal and all was well with us. But it is not. It is perilous. Secular thinkers surveying the world scene recognize the disastrous mess we are making of things. And the Bible makes it abundantly plain. But God's grace to all whom he has made takes priority of place. I always preach about sin in some shape or form when I am preaching the gospel, but I very rarely start from there, and I am cautious about using the word itself, at any rate without very careful explanation. Why so? Because, to the average person today, 'sin', if it means anything at all, refers to sex, murder, or something of the sort. But that is not how the Bible views sin. It is not a moralistic but a theological reality, the disease which has afflicted the whole human race.

Why is it so difficult?
We've already seen that modern people in the West have outgrown Europe's Christian roots. Sin and salvation, heaven and hell, seem the outdated and pessimistic relics of a bygone age. Today we are not bothered by past failures: we are proud of present achievements and drawn by future hopes. We have come of age, and can leave these infantile ideas behind. And that is precisely what liberal theologians and preachers have been doing for some time. The Episcopal Church in the United

States is a prime example. You would be hard put to hear anything about human guilt or the atoning work of Christ in most of its churches. Instead, you will hear of total inclusivity as the great mark of the church: all lifestyles are acceptable. Repentance is not called for. And Jesus, if he ever existed, was a good man and a fine teacher, but nothing more. They have forgotten, or deliberately rejected, the classical biblical truths of sin, the atonement, and the bodily resurrection of Jesus. Instead, they have majored on issues less controversial to modern people, such as inclusivity, justice, millennial goals and so forth. This is a well-intentioned, but flawed, attempt to make the gospel acceptable. The hard parts are left out, particularly the tough, but necessary, message about human sin and divine redemption.

A good few years ago, I was invited to speak at a conference for the leaders of the United Methodist denomination in America. They were worried by the decline in their numbers and their reluctance to evangelize. So I spoke on evangelism and stressed that, if we were to be faithful to the New Testament gospel, we could not hide the unpalatable truth of human sin and our inability by ourselves to get through to a holy God. One night they had a special guest, the famous preacher from the Crystal Cathedral, no less! As I listened to this eloquent man, I became more and more uncomfortable. What he was saying was a reinforcement of the human potential movement: humans have within them all that is necessary to get us to God and live a victorious Christian life. Sin was entirely left out of the glowing picture he was painting. So I reluctantly felt I had to counteract this heresy, for such it was, when I got up to speak the next morning. Not an easy thing to do! But you never really appreciate grace until you recognize the depths of sin.

In contrast to this liberal emasculation of the gospel message, evangelicals have often tended to be lukewarm about social and political aspirations, but have concentrated in their preaching on individual guilt and redemption, often using those very terms. Unfortunately they do not resonate with the culture of today. 'Who has the right to tell me I am guilty?' people might well exclaim. 'On the contrary, I live a pretty good life. And why should I believe the Christian story of redemption, when there are so many other religions available, and, better still, the fashionable and attractive agnosticism which absolves me from thinking about such things at all?'

What does the Bible mean by sin?
Sin is rather a complex idea, but the Bible does not so much focus on individual *sins* as on the fundamental *sin* underlying them all. The Bible does not concern itself primarily with individual acts of sin, either of omission or commission, but rather with our sinful state before God, our underlying condition. And just as an illness has visible symptoms, so the state of sin produces visible sinful actions. And just as all doctors know that it is pointless to treat symptoms if they neglect the root cause, so evangelists know that they have to address the state of sin, rather than merely the individual sinful actions. Sin is the state of alienation from God. We are all born into that flawed humanity. But this flaw was not created by God; it is the result of human rebellion against God, deeply rooted in everyone. It expresses itself at every level of human existence: personal, social, as well as in the structures of society.

At the personal level, people experience this dislocation from the way God made us in a variety of ways. Many folk are plagued by the dread of death. Others are more aware of an unfulfilled yearning for something indefinable which no created object can satisfy. Others are haunted by a sense of guilt, usually because of some serious wrongdoing in the past. In others, this state of sin comes out in frustration, the inability to achieve what they aim for, the falling short of their highest ideals. In others, it shows up in a desire to be totally independent of God, denying his existence and ignoring what he requires of us. Such, at the personal level, are some aspects of the 'sin' which underlies and gives rise to our 'sins'.

At the social and structural levels, sin shows itself in the radical selfishness we see all around us. Self-interest, without care for other people, expresses itself all over the world as the dark side of human nature. Good policies flounder because of the greed or corruption of those entrusted with carrying them out. This greed is wrecking the environment. You don't need the Bible to tell you that there is a basic flaw in human nature – it is perfectly obvious, affecting all our policies and the very environment in which we live. The problems of the world – nuclear, climatic, racial and a host of others – are too great for anyone to handle. As a race, we have proved time and again that we are unable to achieve our good intentions. The great liberal dream was that education would produce a race of enlightened and selfless individuals who would do all for the common good, in their determination to construct a better world. But it has not worked out like that, has it? You have only to reflect on the Soviet ideal of equality for all – and the greed and corruption of the senior ranks in their government, whose job it was to bring about this desirable result. And the Christian gospel is concerned, not with wrong actions as such, so much as a wrong relationship with God: the heart of our predicament. The Greek in which our New Testament was written makes it plain that *hamartia* (singular, 'sin') rather than *hamartiai* (plural, 'sins') is our root problem. Our alienation from God must be addressed if our situation is to be transformed.

The language the New Testament uses to bring this home is varied and instructive. We read of *hamartia*, missing the mark, *parabasis*, crossing the line, *akrasia*, the inability to control ourselves, and *anomia*, lawlessness or raising our fist against God. In short, I believe the New Testament offers us four major ways of understanding sin, and they may help us both to understand and to communicate the subject in a relevant way to our contemporaries.

What is sin?

1. **Sin is an illness**, a chronic illness. It implies a loss of health, a state of weakness and deterioration that leads inexorably to death. The Greek verb *sōzein*, 'to save', has the basic meaning of 'make whole, heal'. That in itself shows the close link between salvation and healing. With this understanding in mind, Augustine long ago saw the church as a hospital, full of people who knew they were ill and needed help, and had turned to Christ to heal them. Sin is like a genetic disorder we are born with, and there is only one doctor who can handle it.

2. **Sin is moral guilt**. It puts us in the wrong with God. It is not difficult to see that God must by definition be holy, and we are not. He is righteous, and we fall far short of that righteousness. The basic idea here is of missing the target, failing

to reach the standard. We know what God expects of us, and we fall short of it. Salvation includes, as one of its main components, the idea of cancelling moral guilt, forgiving that falling short.

> He was pierced for our transgressions,
>   he was crushed for our iniquities;
> the punishment that brought us peace was upon him,
>   and by his wounds we are healed.
> (Isaiah 53:5)

3. **Sin is an enslaving force**. It is like a muddy swamp into which we sink, and we find ourselves trapped. It is like an electromagnet, holding us tightly, as if we were iron filings. Someone has to turn the current off if we are to be set free. It is like gravity that drags everything down. We need a stronger force if we are to be lifted up. It is like a drug, and we cannot break the habit. One of the finest descriptions of this is given by the apostle Paul, acutely conscious of his inability to control the forces that pull him down (Romans 7:13–25). He concludes: 'What a wretched man I am! Who will rescue me from this body of death? Thanks be to God – through Jesus Christ our Lord!'

4. **Sin is existential alienation**. Heidegger, the existentialist philosopher back in the 1930s, distinguished two ways to live: inauthentic or authentic existence. The former is a fallen way, failing to achieve our potential. The latter is fulfilling, in which we achieve our full stature as human beings. The post-war French existentialists such as Camus, Sartre and Simone de Beauvoir developed this contrast, and the New Testament is

strong on it, with its brilliant imagery of living in darkness or light, sin or grace, death or life, being lost or being found. There are just two ways to live: one we foolishly choose and get gripped by, the other a free gift through the death and resurrection of Jesus. In evangelism, I often use quotations from these existentialist writers, with their sense of lostness and despair, which connect with so many people today and contrast so powerfully with the offer of Christ.

I think of an able existentialist whom the local students deemed impervious to the gospel. He came to Christ with joy and gratitude once he found himself understood. There was no need for me to talk to him about the human predicament (which the Christian students had been doing assiduously anyway). He was well aware of it. He needed to understand, within his frame of reference, that faith was not a leap into the dark, but a step into the light; that openness to the ultimate experience was not suicide, but entry into a new dimension of being. Supremely, he needed to come into an I–Thou relationship with Jesus. He did so, and became a fine Christian man.

So how can we proclaim this biblical understanding of sin today?

I think the secret of proclaiming this is to reflect on current examples in our culture which can make some aspect of the New Testament teaching crystal clear. We need to have one foot in the biblical revelation and the other in the contemporary culture. Newspapers, films, TV news and current pop songs are great resources. Is someone captured by terrorists and held to ransom? Does some apparently healthy person turn out to have unsuspected cancer spreading through their body? Does a world-famous golfer have a secret life which drags him into disrepute, once it becomes known? Does a fine, flourishing tree crash to the ground in a storm and you find that, all unseen, rot has been setting in for years? Do we read, as we have done in the UK recently, that hospital treatments of alcohol-related problems have run into millions of pounds and could well bankrupt the National Health Service? All such news items are grist to our mill as preachers.

But there are certain areas on which we will particularly want to reflect, and build into our evangelistic preaching. We touched on some of them at the end of chapter 4.

One is *alienation*. Countless people feel it. Alienated from a spouse, from family, even from self. Many feel alienated from decision-making at work, and from government, which is why so many do not even bother to vote. The preacher can point out that we *feel* alienated precisely because we *are* alienated. Fundamentally, we are alienated from God, and that is the origin of all the other alienations.

Another way into many hearts is to explore the nature of *emptiness*. Many people who seem to have everything are dissatisfied, deep down. Think of Kurt Cobain, the millionaire lead singer of Nirvana, who killed himself several years ago because, although he had a baby in the next room, he could not bear to live with himself any longer: 'I'm a stain. I'm so ugly. I hate myself, and I want to die.' Sadly, he had his wish. Such stories are commonplace. They provide an easy way to speak of human sin, even though it may be hidden from most observers by wealth and fame. Prince Charles put it well: 'There remains in the soul, if I may use such a word, the persistent and unconscious anxiety that something is missing

– something that makes life worth living.' The evangelist can work with that sense of emptiness.

Closely allied to this feeling of emptiness is the *lack of meaning* which so many people find in their lives. They have short-term purposes, of course: to collect the children from school, to make the dinner, and so on. But if you ask them whether they see any long-term purpose in life, they are apt either to doubt it or deny it. A few, such as the musician John Cage, are happy to live with that. 'The highest purpose is to have no purpose at all,' he wrote, and this is apparent in his music. But most people get profoundly depressed by the lack of purpose and meaning in life. Hear the Nobel prize-winner Jacques Monod in his book *Chance and Necessity*: 'The universe is not pregnant with life nor the biosphere with meaning. Our number came up in the Monte Carlo game.'[1] Or go back to the existentialists. Sartre saw no meaning or purpose in life. He wrote in *Nausea*, 'Every existent being is born without reason, prolongs itself out of weakness, and dies by chance.'[2] Camus reflects, 'This world has no importance. Once a man realizes this, he wins his freedom. Or does he? What is intolerable is to see man's life drained of meaning, to be told there is no reason for living.'[3] Once again, this awareness of people's sense of meaningless-ness is a marvellous opening for the sensitive evangelist. If the pessimistic atheism of Sartre and the somewhat more cheerful atheism of Camus leave us bereft of meaning, would we not be wise to return to the God who provides meaning and purpose for life?

Another approach is to examine the current search, obvious in many quarters, for *something more in life*. It is fascinating

to realize that this has flowered in an age when material pos-
sessions have never been so plentiful. There is still a hunger for
'something more'. But the pursuit of happiness so often proves
elusive. Some of the richest individuals I have known have also
been among the most miserable. Maybe this basic human
experience is trying to tell us something, to point us to
something we do not yet know, but which is hinted at by what
we do know. It is as if there is something which lies beyond us
that exercises a hidden attraction upon us, like the fragrance
of a flower we have never smelt, or a visitor from a land we
have never met. Alexander Solzhenitsyn puts it well:

> We are sometimes sent – indistinctly, briefly – revelations not
> to be achieved by rational thought. It is like that small mirror
> in the fairy tales – you glance in it and what you see is not
> yourself: for an instant you glimpse the Inaccessible where no
> horse or magic carpet can take you. And the soul cries out for it.

But many people today are *blind* to their state before God.
Sometimes a story helps the preacher in this situation. In *La
Symphonie Pastorale*, André Gide tells the moving story of a
blind girl in Switzerland.[4] Her pastor tries to convey to her
the beauty of the Alps, the brilliant colours of the flowers, the
majesty of snow-capped mountains. However, he is constantly
frustrated by the limitations of language. But an eye surgeon
in Lausanne believes he can operate and restore her sight. He
is successful, and for the first time in her life she can see. 'When
you gave me my sight,' she says, 'my eyes opened on a world
more beautiful than I had ever dreamed it could be. I had never
imagined that the daylight was so bright, the air so brilliant

and the sky so vast.' The reality far exceeded what the pastor had described, though his words were in fact clues to what she later discovered. A story like this can bring home to people their blindness to spiritual truth, which nothing less than a divine operation can transform, so that they experience it for themselves. This blindness, combined with longing, is another way to preach 'sin' to people today.

However, perhaps the greatest failing of the Western world is our *materialism*. This too can be a way in for the evangelist who is seeking to open people's eyes to the fact that they have everything to live with, but nothing to live for. There are many biblical stories which make this plain. Perhaps the most pungent is the rich fool in Luke's Gospel (12:16–21), a man with no fear of God before his eyes, who suddenly has a heart attack and all his dreams of prosperity are dashed. The only ironic question is who is going to inherit the wealth he has accumulated. God's verdict on his tombstone is succinct: 'You fool!'

I remember a conversation with Andrew Lloyd Webber and Tim Rice, the creators of musicals, including the celebrated *Joseph and the Amazing Technicolor Dreamcoat*. We had been discussing the truth of Christianity on radio, and at greater length in the green room afterwards. I started a correspondence with one of them, and, although it was years ago, I still remember one poignant sentence from it: 'Michael, I haven't become a Christian yet, but I can affirm from personal experience that making a million brings zero satisfaction.' Sadly, I do not think he has ever invested in the heavenly riches offered by Christ.

Another passage that I have found particularly effective in combating materialism is to trace the successive attempts at satisfaction in Ecclesiastes 1 and 2. The man here tries intellectual pursuits, wealth, humour, drink, property, man-management and sex, but he remains empty, and the repeated refrain is:

> Everything was meaningless, a chasing after wind;
>   nothing was gained under the sun.
> (Ecclesiastes 2:11)

It is only in the final chapter of the book that we get a glimpse of the answer:

> Remember your Creator in the days of your youth,
> before the days of trouble come
>   and the years approach when you will say,
>   'I find no pleasure in them.'
> (Ecclesiastes 12:1)

Materialism is false, because, for one thing, people matter more than things. For another, it is addictive: the more you have, the more you want. The Romans had a motto about it: 'Money is like seawater. The more you drink, the thirstier you get.' Materialism hardens the sympathies: compassion flies out of the window when we make money our god. What is more, materialism is self-defeating. For there is in the human heart, as we have already seen, an emptiness that nothing transient can ever fill. No, materialism does not satisfy, and it does not last – we cannot take our money with us. We shall leave it all behind, and, with it, an increasingly devastated planet that we have raped in the pursuit of our gain. Materialism is destructive of all that is best in our characters, and it spells disaster for the world too. It should not be difficult for the evangelist to evoke what, in old-fashioned language, we should call 'conviction of sin' on this matter.

These are some of the ways in which we can bring the human condition of alienation from God and bondage to our self-centredness home to people. We need two things: one, a clear understanding of the fundamental biblical teaching about the nature of sin, and our condition before God; and the second, an imagination which seeks to express this truth in the clothes that people actually wear, the attitudes they consciously or unthinkingly adopt. Make notes of situations in the press, in films, on TV and in pop music which can be useful as you aspire to spread the gospel. Like our Master, we need both biblical fidelity and imaginative flexibility. Then we will find that men and women, even in this post-Christian and post-modern age, are often brought low before the God they have affected to despise.

Chapter 11

THE CROSS REVISITED

The cross has always been a stumbling block. It was so in the first days of the new faith. Jews could not accept that their messiah ended up in the place not only of failure, but also of God's curse (Deuteronomy 21:23). Equally, Gentiles could not accept that anyone who ended up on a criminal's cross could be worthy of worship. And so it has always been. It is easy to understand this scornful rejection of the cross of Christ. Imagine us all going round with a model guillotine or electric chair round our necks, and displayed prominently in our churches. The cross is no less scandalous than that. And yet evangelists down through the ages have taken enormous pride in that terrible cross, and have proclaimed it fearlessly and confidently as God's way of rescuing sinners. 'I resolved to know nothing while I was with you,' wrote the apostle Paul to the Corinthians, 'except Jesus Christ and him crucified;' 'For the message of the cross is foolishness to those who are perishing, but to us who are being saved it is the power of God' (1 Corinthians 2:2; 1:18). All evangelists would say 'Amen' to that.

And yet in today's secular and increasingly anti-Christian society it is not surprising that attacks on the cross should intensify. For example, the Christian doctrine of the atonement is denounced as 'child abuse'. In response to such caricatures, we need to present the full-orbed biblical teaching about the cross with care and clarity.

The cross in the hand of the preacher

It is a great privilege to be entrusted with passing on to others the priceless message of the cross of Christ. But as years go by, we can tend to lose our freshness and develop just one understanding of the wonder of Calvary. That would be to impoverish our message. The New Testament uses many pictures, and so should we.

Jesus the substitute

The whole Bible makes it plain that God and sin cannot mix. Sin brings about a spiritual death, which is why people feel God is so far away: their sins separate them from him. But Jesus went to Calvary to share, and so remove, our alienation. He was our substitute. He came to take the place of sinners, although he was the Son of God, so that we, though sinners, might share his place as sons of God.

But why was it necessary for Christ to die on a cross, that very un-Jewish means of execution? Because to be exposed and hanged on a cross was seen as resting under God's curse (Deuteronomy 21:23). Paul tells the Galatians that all of us lie under God's curse (or righteous judgment) for having broken his law (3:10), and three verses later exclaims, with triumphant joy, that 'Christ redeemed us from the curse of the law, by becoming a curse for us, for it is written: "Cursed is everyone who is hung on a tree"' (Galatians 3:13). You could not possibly explain the idea of substitution more clearly than that! Because he was human, it was humankind's load that he carried. Because he was divine, the consequences of that sin-bearing are limitless and valid for ever. No wonder the Church Fathers wax lyrical on the subject. 'He came for this purpose, that he who was free from sin and altogether holy, should die for sinners,' says Tertullian. 'The Son of God did not disdain to take the flesh of man, and although he was not a sinner, himself to carry the sins of others,' exclaimed Cyprian. 'He underwent judgment to liberate those who were under judgment,' said Augustine. As we know, this wonderful truth brings freedom to the enslaved, self-respect to the down-trodden, cleansing to the guilty, and the blessing of a conscience clean at last. The idea of Christ our substitute is fundamental, and particularly helpful in evangelism. It enables us to see how God could be both 'just and the one who justifies those who have faith in Jesus' (Romans 3:26). It shows us that, what we could never achieve, he has achieved. He has put us in the right with God. But it is not the only understanding of the cross.

Jesus the ransom
Jesus himself said that his life would provide 'a ransom for many' (Mark 10:45). And it did. The early Fathers made much of this image too, because, in those rough days, people were constantly being captured and held to ransom. So it was easy to see the forces of sin and Satan holding people in bondage

until a costly ransom was paid. This particular understanding of the cross fell out of use for a long time, partly because social conditions changed, and partly because people started asking to whom the ransom was paid – perhaps to Satan? This was a classic example of taking a metaphor too far. However, the idea of the ransom is highly appropriate now in these days of hijacking, and I have found that to explain the cross as a ransom, setting captives free at great cost, is readily understood and makes a very effective evangelistic approach.

Jesus the trailblazer

The New Testament shows us in a number of ways that Jesus, through his death and resurrection, has blazed a trail into the very presence of God for us to follow. This is an important aspect of the cross that we tend to neglect. But people today often feel lonely and cut off, excluded from the places of decision-making and power. 'There is no way out, or round, or through,' concluded H. G. Wells in his last book, *Mind at the End of Its Tether*. Well, the cross shows us that there is a way through.

Paul takes up the theme with his wonderful word *prosagōgē*: 'access'. In Romans 5:2, he imagines God as a great king and Jesus as heir to the throne. In our own name, we would never have a chance of access, but Jesus takes us by the hand, leads us past the guards and into the very presence of the Father. Access! What a superb understanding of the cross.

Mark has his own way of making the point. When in 15:37 he records the death of Jesus, he immediately takes us away from Calvary to the temple, and tells us that the great temple curtain was ripped in two from top to bottom. It existed as a sort of 'no entry' sign, to keep people out of the Holy of Holies. Only the high priest could enter, on the Day of Atonement. But when Jesus died, the way to God was split open for all to enter. And at once Mark takes us back to Calvary and the centurion's confession: 'Surely this man was the Son of God.' Here is the first Gentile believer entering the Holy of Holies. The first free access to God's presence is offered to the man who had slain his Son. Abundant access indeed! But that is what God is like. And it makes awesome good sense to those who feel themselves 'outsiders', once they realize it.

Jesus the reconciler

This is an approach which speaks to today's widespread breakdown of relationships at home, at work and between nations. The Greek word for 'reconcile', *katallassō*, means something rather different in the New Testament from today's usage. With us, 'to reconcile' means to find a compromise solution so that two parties can work together. Not so in the New Testament. Reconciliation with God is entirely his gift. We cannot bargain for it. We either accept it or reject it. 'When we were God's enemies, we were reconciled to him through the death of his Son' (Romans 5:10).

There is no compromise on either side in this reconciliation. Both sides make a clear and decisive act of will. God wills to shoulder our debts. Humanity wills to surrender to grace. That is the reconciliation, so costly for him, so free for us, which the cross offers. In any reconciliation, the mediator has to be in harmony with both sides. At the cross we see Jesus in complete solidarity both with humanity and with God, and thus reconciling the world to himself at unspeakable personal cost. Clearly this is a useful approach for evangelists in today's fragmented society.

Jesus the conqueror

The supreme paradox of Calvary is that it looked like defeat, but was in fact victory. The highest place in the universe belongs to self-sacrificial love, and that is what we see at the cross, particularly in St John's account. This aspect of the cross receives much attention in the book of Revelation. Written against a background of anti-religious secularism, not unlike our situation today, it concentrates our gaze on the throne of God. The Lord is in control. The Lamb with the marks of slaughter upon him is on the divine throne. No wonder the redeemed break out in adoration, 'You are worthy' (5:9). For nothing is greater than self-sacrificing love. Nothing can obliterate it. Nothing ever has.

Today's evangelists need to learn from the first Christians, who portrayed Jesus as reigning from the tree. He is the ultimate victor over suffering, evil, the devil and death itself. 'Do not be afraid,' he says to us. 'I am the First and the Last. I am the Living One; I was dead, and behold I am alive for ever and ever! And I hold the keys of death and Hades' (Revelation 1:17–18). What a conqueror! How appropriate for people who are defeated by addictions, crushed under a sense of guilt, in bondage to drugs, drink and the occult, or oppressed by the fear of death. *Christus Victor*, Christ the Conqueror, should be the burden of our message.

Jesus the magnet

To the enquiring Greeks who came in search of him, Jesus said, 'I, when I am lifted up from the earth, will draw all men to myself' (John 12:32). Not all without exception, of course, but all without distinction. His death for their life would be the great magnet to draw people of all types and nationalities to himself. 'Christ's love compels us,' cried Paul in response, 'because we are convinced that one died for all' (2 Corinthians 5:14).

The human heart hungers for love, and the love of God magnetizes the human heart. All through the ages, some Christians have followed Abelard and stressed the magnetic power of the cross to evoke love in our cold hearts, and bring us to God, while others have followed Anselm in stressing the perfect satisfaction and reparation which the cross displayed. Both are needed. Both are true. Evangelists will want to proclaim the joyful news of a substitute for our sins. But they must never fail to allow the sheer grace of Christ crucified and risen to shine out winsomely from their preaching. If people see that the Lord of the universe loved them enough to die for them, that will draw people of all backgrounds to him. The evangelist needs to kneel before the cross until it calls forth tears of gratitude. Then he or she must proclaim it as God's supreme gift to sinners: Christ's arms outstretched on the cross to block the way to hell and welcome back the prodigals. And that leads us to our final section.

The cross in the heart of the preacher

I have been very struck this year when preaching about the wise men who visited the infant Jesus. The Jerusalem clergy of the day knew all about Micah's prophecy; they were clear where the promised Saviour would be born, but they did not go the few miles to Bethlehem to worship him. They did not move a muscle. That is the perennial danger of those who deal in holy things: knowing it all, but not acting upon it.

When taking missions in South Africa, I came across the description of their clergy as signposts, because they pointed the way, but did not follow it! That is always a danger for evangelists. We have grown over-familiar with our message. We almost take the cross for granted. We speak of it as a commodity to be held out to our hearers. We no longer treat it with wonder and awe. When that happens, we are in great danger. The Christian preacher must never be so taken up with a clinical study of the atonement, or bored by a mechanical way of proclaiming it, that he or she cannot marvel with St Paul that 'the Son of God . . . loved me, and gave himself for me' (Galatians 2:20). As a wise friend observed, 'If you want to preach the cross, you'd better stay close to it.'

Actually it cuts even deeper than this. For one of the most profound understandings of the cross is that Jesus is our representative, as well as our substitute. Christ, my substitute, did in my place what I could never do for myself. But Christ my representative does in me what I too must do as a Christian. His death is a pointer to the path I must take. I must die to sin and live for righteousness (1 Peter 2:24). This truth goes back to the teaching of Jesus. In Mark 8 he astonishes his followers, first by telling them that he must go to the cross, and then by asserting that they too must deny themselves, take up their cross, and follow him. Where the head of the new humanity goes, the body must follow.

To put it bluntly, the cross and resurrection are not exclusively events outside of us. They must have their counterpart in our own lives. We have, St Paul tells us, to 'carry around in our body the death of Jesus, so that the life of Jesus may also be revealed in our body' (2 Corinthians 4:10). There has to be a sort of death at work in us if there is to be life for those we serve. There is a throne and a cross in every believer's life. Either Christ is still on the cross and our own self is on the throne, or else we deliberately and daily enthrone him and ask him to keep our old sinful nature on the cross. Dying and rising are the secret of holy living. And without them, we shall have no power in our lives and ministries. Paul takes us deep into this mystery in Romans 6:

> Don't you know that all of us who were baptised into Christ Jesus were baptised into his death? We were therefore buried with him through baptism into death in order that, just as Christ was raised from the dead through the glory of the Father, we too may live a new life.
> (Romans 6:3–4)

Our baptism unites us with Christ, plunging us into his death and resurrection. And Paul draws the consequences in the verses that follow, which can conveniently be summarized under three imperatives: 'Know . . . reckon . . . yield.'

'We know,' says the apostle (6:6), 'that our old self was crucified with him, so that . . . we should no longer be slaves to sin.' The crucifixion of Jesus sounded the death-knell of selfish humanity. It spelt the doom of the sin-infected 'self' which plagues us all. Christians are meant to know that a cosmic battle was won on the cross. The last Adam succeeded where the first Adam failed. His victory potentially involves us all.

It is one thing to know this in our heads. But it is quite another to count or 'reckon' on it (verse 11). But if I do not reckon on it, I cannot enjoy the victory he has made possible. I need to face the pressures arising from my base desires, confident that Christ has dealt them their death-blow at Calvary, and that I need not succumb to them unless I wish to. I have to say 'No' to the temptation: 'I reckon that you have no rights over me, and you shall have no power over me. Christ defeated you at Calvary. I consider myself dead to your blandishments, and alive to God. In the power of the cross I confront you.'

Then, I must offer or 'yield' (verse 13). It is the call for unconditional surrender of myself, my ambitions, my lusts to Christ. There is no need for sin to go on reigning in my body, though it will never be eliminated this side of the grave. If total surrender to Jesus is my clear direction, sin may well trip me up from time to time, but it will no longer tyrannize me. I need to renew that attitude of surrender daily.

Know, reckon, yield! Such is the pathway to that dying to sin and rising to new life to which we are called by our baptism. I wonder, if you have been disappointed by fruitlessness in evangelism recently, whether you have not been treading that path of full surrender? Are there areas of your life you are holding back from Christ? Are there sins you are holding on to? Are there relationships you have no business maintaining? Is there pride that needs to be broken? Then come back to the cross, the cross that brought you new life, the cross you preach to others, and ask the dear Lord to fill you afresh with wonder at his sacrifice, as you lay down all the rubbish you have accumulated. Take it all to the cross. Then you will find a new joy and power in your Christian ministry. I know this is true, because I have so often had to tread and retread that humbling path myself.

Let me end with a story against myself. I preached evangelistically some years ago in Manchester, and there was a substantial response. Some people waited twenty minutes or more in the aisle to come and tell me that they had entrusted their lives to Christ. A few years later, I preached much the same sermon in another part of the country. I do not often repeat sermons, but I did so on this occasion. And nobody responded; nobody was converted. The reason? I think it was because I was consciously holding on to something that was wrong in my life, and it robbed me of joy in my heart and effectiveness in evangelism. Could it be like that with you?

Chapter 12

PREACHING FOR A VERDICT

The job of the evangelist is to electrify the fence on which people are sitting! It is to challenge them to respond to the gospel. But it is a very delicate task, and one that we can easily mess up. We are not selling washing powder – we are dealing with the living God, and with people's souls.

Preparing to preach or speak evangelistically
There are preachers, often Calvinists, who worthily lay out the heart of the gospel and leave it at that, confident that God will do the calling himself, and that it is not for them to intrude. There are others, often Arminians, who are strong on an extensive appeal, sometimes seeking to stir up emotions to maximize numbers, but they have not given sufficient content or apologetic in their talk for people to make a considered decision. I try to avoid either extreme. I am a Calvinist when I am on my knees before an evangelistic talk: the Lord knows

who will come, and who will be ready to respond. It is all his work. But I am an Arminian when I am preaching, calling folk to repent and believe, to commit themselves to the Saviour, just as Jesus challenged people to follow him when he was on earth. I have no idea who will respond, but I want to make the offer available to all.

A good evangelistic talk is crisp: it wastes no words. It is interesting. It grabs attention from the start and maintains it throughout. It is biblical: Scripture has a power that our words do not have. It is relevant to the needs of the hearers, and they know it. Finally, it challenges people to decide.

Often the evangelist will begin by intriguing his (or her) hearers, go on to subvert their wrong ideas of Christianity, explain from the Bible the heart of the gospel, and conclude with a challenge. He will make sure his aim is single and clear. He may not begin with a verse from the Bible, but he will be sure his message is biblical. He will create a clear plan, so clear that nobody can miss it. His illustrations will be gripping. His start and conclusion will both be critical. What is more, the preacher needs to pay attention to his language. Words matter to the Holy Spirit and they should matter to us too: evocative words that can bring home a familiar truth in a fresh way. He will also need to watch his manner, and avoid distracting mannerisms. He is an ambassador, a herald, a servant of the Word, a witness, God's steward – the New Testament gives us all these descriptions. Different styles are appropriate for different situations. The wise evangelist will be utterly Christ-centred in what he or she has to say. Preachers need to make clear who Jesus is, what he has done for us, and the fact that he is alive and can be met today.

Finally, it is important to leave time to conclude. It is all too easy to expand your material as you go along, and then find that, when you come to the end of your talk and need more time, that time has flown. Careful preparation will help with this problem, and give you confidence as you go into the pulpit. It may help to write out the whole talk sometimes, so as to guide you in getting over the tricky transition points that occur in almost every sermon.

Not that you should read an evangelistic address, but the very writing of it has etched it clearly in your mind, and it is a help to have the text there in front of you, should you need it. It is not a bad idea to speak in front of a mirror occasionally, to see what you look like when preaching, and it is valuable, and often humbling, to get a small group in the congregation to meet with you occasionally and assess your clarity, manner, content, illustration and application. Time yourself as you go through the sermon in preparation, and remember that it will always take longer on the day!

But the most important essential in preparation is prayer. In prayer you tell God that you cannot bring about the new birth, however brilliant you may be. Only God can do it. That is why prayer is so important. It tells God that we depend entirely on his working. So get church members to pray for you during the week when you are preparing a major address. Make it a topic of prayer at the prayer meeting. Prayer burns the message into you, and prayer will burn it into the souls of some of your hearers. The Holy Spirit is free to work powerfully in an atmosphere of prayer. He inspired the very Scripture you are going to preach. He guided you as you worked on it. It is his task to commend it to the hearts and wills of your hearers. And prayer enables the Holy Spirit to do just that.

I, for one, go into the pulpit with much greater confidence when two or three of my colleagues gather round me to pray, during the hymn before the sermon. It is an open demonstration that we depend upon God, not on our own efforts. I love the words of the old Methodist lay preacher: 'First, I reads meself full. Then I thinks meself clear. Then I prays meself hot. Then I lets go!'

Concluding an evangelistic address in church

I only offer a challenge to commitment when there has been a clear and reasonably rounded presentation of the gospel. Human need, the cross and resurrection, the cost of discipleship and the availability of the Holy Spirit must at least be touched on, though we obviously cannot major on each one every time.

Here are some of the points I aim to remember.

- If I am going to call for an explicit response, I prefer to have explained what I am going to do earlier on, before I do it, so that it does not come as a shock to people, and render them mentally unprepared to respond. Usually there is some time in the proceedings when announcements are made, and a very matter-of-fact notice like this alerts people to what may follow: 'From time to time, we explain the way to a personal faith at the end of a sermon. We will be doing that today.' Enough said.
- I make it plain that I am interested not primarily in decisions, but in discipleship. This was what Jesus and

his apostles called people to. I have no patience with
those shallow evangelists who aim to get hands raised to
'receive Christ', when it has not been properly explained
what this entails, and when no attempt is made to
gather names or provide aftercare. 'When Christ calls a
man,' said Dietrich Bonhoeffer, 'he bids him come and
die.' It is that serious. If the long-term implications of
the desired response are not spelt out, all we will get are
shallow professions of conversion that melt away before
the next day dawns.

- I am open to the possibility of pleading with people
  to turn to Christ. There is a lot of that loving, pleading
  compassion in the Bible, but I find little of it around
  today. Many preachers just tell you how it is, and
  then stop. It hardly seems to matter to them whether
  you respond or not. That is very different from Jesus:
  'O Jerusalem, Jerusalem . . . how often I have longed
  to gather your children together, as a hen gathers her
  chicks under her wings, but you were not willing'
  (Matthew 23:37). It is impossible to miss the note of
  pleading here. We need to allow the warmth of Jesus,
  the seriousness of the issues, and the awesome alternative
  to coming to Christ to be reflected in what we say at
  this point.
- I seek to kindle the imagination, one way or another,
  and reach the citadel of the will. I am not simply out to
  win the intellect, though that is important, nor to stir
  the emotions, though that may happen. I am aiming for
  the will, the place where serious decision for the long
  term is made.

- I watch people's faces and try to read their minds. This is
  not as difficult as it might seem. Learn to give a succinct
  answer to the questions which you sense may be on their
  minds: 'Are you wondering what it will cost you to
  follow Christ? Good. Let me try to answer that
  question.' Or '"But, Dr Green," you may be thinking,
  "I am a regular churchgoer!"' Your brief reply might be:
  'No doubt, but so too were the Pharisees, whom Jesus
  exposed so devastatingly. Probably even better
  churchgoers than you!' – with a cheeky smile! This
  divining what is going on in hearts and minds, and
  speaking to it, can be very effective. It can, I think, be
  a spiritual gift from God to the preacher. We should ask
  for it. It is particularly valuable in briefly dispelling the
  objections which crowd in as the challenge becomes
  more and more obvious.
- Our manner should be a mixture. On the one hand, we
  need to be fearless and bold. On the other, we need to
  be warm and sensitive. Pray for that balance.
- Trust the Word of God. It is powerful. Placard the
  promises of God and the cross of Christ before the
  eyes of your audience. Faith is, after all, trust in the
  promises of God. These promises may well be very new
  to them. They need time, and you need great clarity, if
  they are to take them on board.
- Use appropriate illustrations at this delicate time, ones
  that illuminate personal relationship. I have found that
  the marriage analogy between the Lord and the believer
  is clear, comprehensible and biblical. It is as though the
  Father says to Jesus something like what the pastor says

to the bridegroom: 'Jesus, will you take this sinner, to
have and to hold from this day forward, for better, for
worse, for richer, for poorer, until not even death can
part you?' Jesus replies, 'I will.' The Father then says to
the sinner, as the pastor then says to the bride, 'Sinner,
will you take this Jesus to have and to hold, from this
day forward, for better, for worse, for richer, for poorer,
until not even death can part you?' The only fitting reply
is: 'I will.' A marriage is not effective until the bride has
given her word of commitment to the groom; neither
is a conversion real until the sinner has pledged his
commitment to the Lord, whose arms have long been
extended to him.

Another personal illustration, found in Revelation
3:20, speaks of our life as a house, and Christ as the
visitor, the Light of the World no less, standing at the
door, asking us to repent and let him in. It is so down to
earth, so natural, that anyone can understand it. Christ
has long been knocking, and the door has remained fast
shut. He is such a gentleman that he will come in only
when invited. The preacher asks his or her hearers, 'If you
have never done so before, will you ask him in now? You
may or may not feel any immediate difference. That is
not the point. He promises that if *anyone* opens the door
(and that must include you) he *will*, not he *may*, come
in. There is no "perhaps" about it. If you ask him, he will
respond, and then the two of you are together in the
house of your life, locked in an indissoluble partnership.'

You may need to explain, in passing, that of course the
physical Christ is back in heaven, but his unseen self, his

Holy Spirit, enters the believer's life and makes Jesus real. This is a particularly powerful image for church people who are unconverted, because this was the situation at Laodicea, to which this message was first sent. The church people thought they were wonderful: rich, prosperous, in need of nothing. Christ's laser eye saw, however, that they were 'wretched, pitiful, poor, blind and naked' (Revelation 3:17). And all because their true provider, the Lord himself, had never been granted access to their lives. It was basically a Christless church at Laodicea, although it had all the paraphernalia of religion. This was a problem that could not be solved en masse, but only as each individual heard the Saviour's voice and invited him in. It is in this context of opening the door to Christ that the language about 'receiving him' makes sense.

Another good biblical response image is that of the seed and the soil, or the sperm and the egg. It is from the union of these two that new life is born. People do not find difficulty in seeing their life as the soil, and Christ's word or Spirit as the divine seed that needs to be implanted, if there is to be any new life. To 'come to Christ' is yet another readily comprehensible picture. So too is 'give and take'. You give yourself to him and you gratefully take his Holy Spirit in return. Do not get yourself boxed into using just one image, because different people are helped by different illustrations for this crucial encounter with Christ.

• You might be wise to be very broad in your appeal at the end of the sermon. There will be a big variety of people in the congregation, many of them already Christians, and you want to be of maximum help to all. You could call people who have never entrusted their lives to Christ to do so, and then add, 'There may well be some who did that long ago. But somehow you have drifted away. Come back to him now. Ask his pardon. Put yourself without reserve into his hands. Be prepared for a life of discipleship, and you will know again the joy you had when first you came to him.' It is sometimes helpful, when people seem genuinely unsure as to whether or not they have come to Christ, to suggest that they ink in whatever pencilled commitment they may have made in the past. So make a broad and challenging appeal. But do not exert pressure. It is the job of the Holy Spirit, not the preacher, to do that. Human pressure can do a lot of damage.

- Usually at the end I suggest a time of silence. Silence is not only golden; it is also powerful. It gives the Spirit of God a chance to speak to individuals. I may well repeat the verse of Scripture that has been foremost in the sermon, and leave one or even two whole minutes of complete silence, inviting people to face up to Christ's call on their lives, and encouraging those who are already Christians to pray silently for those who are not, and to surrender any areas of their lives they may be holding back from the Lord.

I am careful to avoid emotionalism. I try to make it seem the most natural thing in the world to accept Christ gratefully into one's life, or to pray for others to do so. If I am matter-of-fact about it, the congregation will not feel that any illegitimate emotional pressure is being exerted, and the Holy Spirit will be free to do his sovereign work. Often in the silence, people will start to weep. But that is fine. The Holy Spirit is at work in them, and almost invariably this encounter leads them to repentance and the new life.

- After a time of silence, I often suggest a prayer of commitment for those who want to use it, *and only for them*. Many people are unable to verbalize what they want to say to God. So I might say, 'If you feel you don't know how to put it, why not use something very simple like this? You could say it after me under your breath if you like. "Lord, please forgive me, and come and take up residence in my life. Change me, and make me your faithful follower for the rest of my days. Amen."' Another prayer I sometimes suggest has the advantage of employing three of the earliest words anyone says: Sorry . . . Thank you . . . Please. 'Lord, I am sorry for the mess I have made in my life, and for having kept you at arm's length for so long. Thank you for dying on the cross for me, and being alive to change me. Please come and take your rightful place in my life. Amen.'

- I then publicly thank God that he keeps his promises and will never forsake the person who has come to him. And before people go, I offer a free book to those who are thinking hard, but are not yet ready to commit themselves, and I ask those who have responded to Christ to come and have a word with me, so that we can sign them up for a nurture course. This should start in the ensuing week. The gathering of fruit in this way is essential. I decline to speak evangelistically unless there is a (prospective) nurture programme in place. I will say more about this in the next chapter.

It is good to train the congregation to turn to their guest at this point and say, 'Would you care to join one of these nurture groups? They are a real help for growing in the Christian life. I'll come with you to the front, if you would like company as you sign up.' I sometimes myself approach a visitor who I can see has been touched by the Holy Spirit and invite him or her to join a group. A tactful word from a staff member on the door can encourage a visitor who is leaving, to go back and sign up for a group! With all this activity going on at the end of the service, it makes it easy for those who want to pray or reflect to stay in their seats. And it makes it easy for your fellow leaders to chat to individuals who may have been affected. Often immediate ministry at this point is invaluable, and information gained can help those who are going to welcome the newcomer into the nurture group.

So far I have not mentioned the use of evangelistic materials. But it helps to have your favourite evangelistic booklet available after the service, so that you can offer it to people who have said 'Yes' to Christ. It gives them something to come and ask for, and therefore lessens the embarrassment of going up for a solo talk with a minister about God! What is more, it will take the readers coherently through the steps to faith, and thus enable them to clarify their decision and understand a bit more about it. The thing to avoid, I think, is equating the taking of a booklet with having put faith in Christ.

At this stage, people may be staggered by the
immensity of what Christ is offering, and the need for
revolution in their lives. They are scarcely in a position
to know whether they have 'accepted Christ' or not. It is
all spinning round in their head. There will be, and there
must be, a proper occasion for publicly confessing
Christ at a future date, but the time is not now! You
want to make it easy for them to get the help which a
clearly written booklet affords, and to make that initial
contact which will bring them into a nurture group,
where these things can be teased out over the next
couple of months.

Concluding an evangelistic talk at a restaurant or in a home

Thus far we have considered evangelism in church. But church
is often the worst place to do it, because the very building
seems a threat to those who never go. Neutral ground is best,
so a restaurant or a home work well. The atmosphere is so
much more friendly, especially if, like Jesus, you do a lot of
your outreach over food. Personally, I much prefer these
occasions to formal preaching in church.

At this evangelistic dinner, breakfast or business lunch,
many of the same principles we have already considered still
apply. You will need an attractive title, printed on an invitation card, which people can give to their friends. You will
need to ensure that the food part of the occasion does not go
on so long that there is little time for the address. But at the
end of the meal, or, better still, before the final course or coffee
(which provides good conversation time after the talk is

given), the chairperson stands up and introduces the speaker, who then gives a talk in the most amusing, clear, winsome and challenging way he or she can. It is often good to end with a challenge. At this point, turn to unmarked cards and pens which have been unobtrusively placed on tables (maybe under a vase of flowers!) beforehand, in sufficient numbers for every person to have one. Ask them all to pick up a card and a pen. Then say, 'I wonder if you would be kind enough to help us? We do not do a lot of events like this, and would love your reactions to what you have experienced today. So could you jot them down for us? You know – "food great, talk awful", or something of the sort! We would also be glad if you could suggest one or two topics that might go down well on another occasion.'

You may need to wait and hold your nerve before the most reluctant ones get writing, but when everyone is hard at it, say, 'By the way, if you have today or recently taken that step of commitment I spoke about, could you just jot down your name and phone number at the bottom of your comments, so that we can invite you to something that will help? All of you, just leave your cards on the table – we will pick them up. And thanks so much for your help.'

I am often surprised at those who leave their names: they would have been most unlikely to come forward at an appeal, but the privacy of just leaving their name works for them.

We need to have the courage to preach for a verdict from time to time. People cannot just drift into the Christian life. They need to decide. And the skilled and loving evangelist can help them to do just that.

Chapter 13

OUR RESPONSIBILITY – AND GOD'S

Our responsibility: the nurture of new Christians
One of the weakest areas in Western Christianity is that it does
not know how to look after new believers. This is partly because
so few churches seem to gain them. And if they do, they might
plug them into an Alpha course (but Alpha is meant for
evangelism, not nurture, and rarely gets their noses into
Scripture). But in general, any new believers are left to their
own devices, to try to cope with the regular church services.
This is scandalous. It is like expecting babies to eat meals of
meat and vegetables when what they need is milk.

The first Christians did not make that mistake. From the
day of Pentecost, they took immense care over nurture.
Acts 2 makes this very plain. They carefully counted those who
professed faith, even though the number (3,000) was so large.
Then they baptized the new converts. They taught them
apostolic doctrine, derived from Jesus, and majored on bringing

them into the apostolic fellowship. They stressed the importance of worship and introduced them to Holy Communion.
They showed them how to make prayer a priority and insisted
on their making a public witness. We see throughout Acts and
the Epistles what care the leaders gave to pastoral oversight,
by personal visits and by letter. So here are nine elements in
Christian nurture which we could expand on at length. They
ought to be carefully considered by every church which hopes
to have new believers in its midst. It is simply unfair to bring
people to the most important decision they will ever make and
then neglect to nourish them into discipleship and fruitful
service of God.

My experience strongly suggests that the best nurture takes
place in a small group, with caring, sensitive leaders. The
group not only feeds the new Christians, but is invaluable in
helping those on the edge of Christian commitment to take
the plunge and then grow. Time and again, I have found
in the many groups I have led in Oxford, Canada, the US and
elsewhere, that some of the members of a new nurture group
had clearly committed themselves, while some had not yet
taken the step, some were not sure where they stood, and some
were drawn by the Spirit of God to sign up without having
even the least idea of why they had done so! But nine weeks
later they were almost always all committed to Christ and on
the path to discipleship. Once the waverers in the group see
other people's faith becoming real, and prayers getting
answered, they are challenged to respond themselves. They
also begin to experience Christian fellowship, and during
the course have the opportunity to make their decision when
they are ready, rather than when the evangelist wants them

to. I cannot emphasize too strongly the importance of the nurture group. Remember, we are not after decisions, but after disciples.

Outline of a nurture course

There are a lot of Christian courses on the market these days, but curiously enough, research has shown that your own local course, carefully tailored to your situation, is slightly more effective than any of these. I have used a simple course in four continents over a number of years. Here it is. Please use it, or adapt it, if you think it can help.

The first session – either one-to-one or in a group – ought to be on the new birth, the new life in Christ which, hopefully, participants will have begun. A suitable passage to examine together would be John 3:1–16, Acts 9:1–19 or Luke 19:1–10. All these contain examples of people coming to new life in Christ. You will want to help the person or the group to see what is the main point of the passage, and learn to draw thoughts from it for their own lives. It would then be good to pray those thoughts in, and to end by discussing the problems that the new believer is sure to experience.

On your second occasion, you might read 1 John 5:1–15. It is all about the grounds for assurance that Christians are meant to enter into. Particularly important is verse 12, and the emphasis that, if you have the Son in your heart, then you have entered into eternal life: it is not merely a future hope. The group will probably be amazed to learn that you can actually know whether you are a Christian or not.

In week three, you might usefully turn up Luke 11:1–13. There is lots of teaching here about prayer, and it would be particularly helpful to show your friends how to use the Lord's Prayer, not simply as something to recite, but as a pattern for their own prayer life. No doubt discussion will follow about examples of answered prayer, and why some prayers remain unanswered.

Week four might well be designed to show the importance of devotional Bible reading. Any part of Psalm 119 would serve your purpose, and so too would Joshua 1:1–10, which is not only a most encouraging Old Testament passage for your friend or friends to taste, but concentrates on the importance of meditating on, and obeying, God's Word if the spiritual life is to be successful. Alternatively, use Matthew 4:1–11, showing how Jesus stored passages from the Scriptures (Deuteronomy, actually, which he had probably recently been studying) in his heart, and how useful this proved in overcoming temptation. In discussion afterwards, you could seek to ensure that your friends have material, such as Scripture Union notes, to help them with their devotional lives of prayer and Bible reading.

The fifth week ought to be on Christian fellowship. Your friend or friends need to see that, although they came to Christ on their own, God's purpose is that they should be part of a fellowship which embodies something of God's kingdom. Passages such as 1 Corinthians 12:1–26 or John 15:1–17 would be good for demonstrating the interconnectedness of Christians and their dependence on the Lord. Your friends are going to need, in addition to the initial discipling by yourself, to be initiated into a small fellowship group and into the church at large.

Week six ought probably to be on the person and work of the Holy Spirit in the life of the Christian. What passage could be better than Romans 8:1–17 for this, or perhaps Galatians 5:16–26? There is so much ignorance about the Holy Spirit that this session is particularly important and should not be hurried, because there are sure to be lots of questions!

Week seven should be on Christian behaviour. The inner working of the Spirit must have its outer manifestation in transformation of life. The Epistles are full of help here. Perhaps choose Colossians 3:1–17, Philippians 4 or Romans 12.

Week eight might be devoted to the important topic of family life, and a passage such as Ephesians 5:21 – 6:9 would be very appropriate.

Finally the new believers need something challenging and exciting about Christian service and living. A passage such as 1 Peter 2:1–11 would be excellent for the final week.

I have suggested nine sessions: basics for new Christians. You do not need any book other than the Bible. You can do this with individuals or a group. But you will want to teach them to feed on the Scriptures. For the Bible is nourishment, without which they certainly will not grow. And the evangelist needs to ensure that some such nurture is in place in the background, before he or she issues a challenge to respond to Christ. I am profoundly grateful to Richard Gorrie who led me to Christ, whom I mentioned in chapter 1, for he took time to meet me regularly and go through passages like those above, enabling me to get my sea legs as a Christian.

God's responsibility: the creation of new life

One of the profound insights throughout the Bible is that human beings, though mentally, physically and socially alive, are spiritually dead. Something snapped in humanity when sin entered the world, cutting us off from intimacy with God. And only God could restore that link.

It is so important for evangelists not to appear like hucksters, selling salvation. All they can do is point to the Lord who can bring people 'from darkness to light, and from the power of Satan to God' (Acts 26:18). To give that new life is God's prerogative, and he does not entrust it to anyone else. Consequently, prayer must be a top priority for the evangelist. In prayer he is saying to God, in effect, 'Lord, I cannot make the spiritually blind to see, and bring the spiritually dead to life. Only you can do it. Please, Lord, exert your sovereign power, and use me if I can be of service to you. If not, act without me!' If that is our attitude, the glory will go where it belongs – to God and not to any human being.

The marvellous thing, though, is that God frequently does use us in a variety of ways. I recently got this letter from Becky Pippert, a very gifted American evangelist. I quote it, with her permission, because it shows a number of elements coming together in evangelism, provided by several Christian agents. But above all, it shows that God is the evangelist.

Becky was recently asked to preach evangelistically in a church in Belfast which many students from Queen's University attend. Unknown to her, Cathy, one of the student leaders at Queen's, felt God was prompting her to invite a man from Bangladesh. She had recently met him and his wife, as they were now living in Belfast. Becky writes, 'But when Cathy called to invite him, he began an angry diatribe over the phone. Full of hostility, he went on for a full twenty minutes. Where was God in the tsunami? Why is there so much suffering?' He explained that he had been raised a Muslim and had practised his faith until he became disenchanted. He described himself as an 'angry secular humanist'. Cathy wisely did not try to defend – she listened. She told him his questions were excellent and needed a careful response. She encouraged him to talk with her pastor – but she asked him to the service anyway. She hung up, discouraged, and questioning whether it really had been God's leading to invite him. Of course, by now she was sure he would never come.

'At the service,' Becky continued, 'I spoke on the resurrection, and I prayed at the end of the sermon for anyone who wanted to commit their life to Christ. Immediately afterwards, the man from Bangladesh approached me. He said, "I came this morning full of anger. I've been a Muslim for most of my life – but in recent years I became an agnostic. I came to hear your talk, so I could tear it apart. But something began to happen. First, I found myself drawn by what you were saying. I could relate to your earlier search for God, and I found your talk thoughtful and well-reasoned. The stories you told from the Bible seemed so real and human. But then something happened. As you were speaking I suddenly saw a great light. It was whiter than white. I can't find the words to describe it because it has never happened to me before. But I knew it was Jesus. And he was telling me to quit fighting him and surrender. So I want you to know, I prayed that prayer with you. I committed my life to Christ this morning. And I meant it."'

Becky continued, 'I took him immediately to the senior pastor, and they talked for quite some time. Just as I was being introduced for the first time to Cathy, the pastor walked up, beaming, and said, "Becky, this is the real deal. He really did commit his life to Christ, and he understood what he was doing. And, as in the case of many Muslims in my experience, God brought conversion through a supernatural vision. I will follow up with him, and he will start a Christianity Explored course this week."'

'Cathy asked us who this person was, and when she heard his name, she burst into tears! Then she proceeded to tell me about the phone call the night before! Can you imagine what a faith-strengthener this was for her? And how it will encourage the whole of the Christian Union at Queen's?'

I received this letter as I was contemplating writing this chapter. It seemed to me an excellent example of the varied human ministries which often contribute to a person's conversion, and the overwhelming divine activity which brings it about. At the human level, there was Cathy's invitation of someone she wanted to hear the gospel. There was her wisdom in courteously enduring a verbal assault without answering back. Then there was the pastor's part. He had an evangelistic heart, laid on a special evangelistic service, and invited a proven evangelist to preach. Moreover, he had a diagnostic talk with the man afterwards, was convinced of the reality of this man's commitment, and introduced him at once into a nurture course.

Becky's part was no less important. She chose a central aspect of the faith on which to preach an evangelistic sermon. It included exposition, reasoned argument, good stories and a strong challenge. At the close, she did not duck out of suggesting a prayer of commitment for those who felt ready. And she was rewarded with a response by several people, but notably the Bangladeshi. She wisely did not spend too much time with him herself, since she was a visitor who would almost immediately be on her way, but introduced him to the senior pastor who would be around for some years. All of these were excellent initiatives on the part of the human agents. They had got it right.

But none of this would have had any effect without the activity of God the Evangelist. It was God who prompted Cathy to invite this man. It was God who gave her the wisdom not to argue when he poured out abuse down the phone. It was God who prompted the man to come. It was God who touched his heart as he heard of Jesus and the resurrection. It was God who gave him this remarkable vision which led him to the new birth. God was the evangelist. Of course, he does not always intervene in such a spectacular manner. In fact, I believe God rarely repeats his actions in drawing people to himself, respecting individuals and drawing them in just the way that is appropriate for them. But always he is the one who brings new life.

I love the short story Jesus once told as he sat with a crowd of disreputable non-churchgoers. You would not find them in the synagogue, these tax gatherers, but they were fascinated by Jesus. And not surprisingly, because he told the most marvellous stories. In this one, he likened God to a woman who had ten silver coins (perhaps from her wedding headdress) and lost just one of them. Instead of remaining satisfied with the nine she still had, the woman was desperate to find this precious coin, and she swept the house with immense care – until she found it. She then gathered her friends and neighbours to tell them the good news, saying, 'Rejoice with me; I have found my lost coin.' 'In the same way,' says Jesus, 'there is rejoicing in the presence of the angels of God over one sinner who repents' (Luke 15:8–10).

A mere three verses, but what an arresting story! The original hearers must have been dumbfounded to hear Jesus liken God to a woman! Maybe their amazement deepened as they imagined the search, some of it no doubt on hands and knees in case the precious coin had fallen down a crack. But that is what God is like. He cares for every single person, and goes to endless lengths to find them. That is the heart of God the Evangelist. And if there is joy on earth – and there certainly is – when one person comes to Christ, it is matched, Jesus tells us, by massive rejoicing in heaven. What a privilege, as an evangelist, to work for and with such a loving, caring, searching God. What a privilege to join in his joy from time to time, as he finds precious individuals who were lost.

NOTES

Chapter 4 What good news?

1. William J. Abraham, *The Art of Evangelism* (Cliff College, 1993).

Chapter 5 Church alive

1. Youth with a Mission.
2. Operation Mobilisation.
3. Michael Green, *Forgotten Dynamite* (Kingsway, 2003).

Chapter 6 University outreach

1. Rebecca Manley Pippert, *Out of the Saltshaker and Into the World* (IVP, new edn 2010).

Chapter 7 Careless talk

1. Michael Green, *The Meaning of Salvation* (Regent College Publishing, 2000).

Chapter 9 Reason to believe

1. Michael Green and Alister McGrath, *Springboard for Faith* (Hodder & Stoughton, 1993), p. 17.
2. Stephen Hawking and Leonard Mlodinow, *The Grand Design* (Bantam, 2010), p. 180.
3. See *Daily Mail*, 3 September 2010.

Chapter 10 Whatever happened to sin?
1. Jacques Monod, *Chance and Necessity: An Essay on the Natural Philosophy of Modern Biology* (Knopf, 1971).
2. Jean-Paul Sartre, *Nausea* (New Direction, 2007; first published 1938).
3. Albert Camus, *Caligula* (Vintage, 1962).
4. André Gide, *La Symphonie Pastorale* (Flammarion, 1996; originally published 1919).